The
Nature of
Holiness

The
Nature of
Holiness

JOHN WESLEY

BETHANY HOUSE PUBLISHERS
MINNEAPOLIS, MINNESOTA 55438
A Division of Bethany Fellowship, Inc.

Published by Bethany House Publishers
A Division of Bethany Fellowship, Inc.
6820 Auto Club Road, Minneapolis, Minnesota 55438

Printed in the United States of America

Library of Congress Cataloging-in-Publication Data

Wesley, John, 1703–1791.
  The nature of holiness.

  (The Wesley library for today's reader)
  1. Methodist Church—Sermons.   2. Holiness—Sermons.
3. Sermons, English. I. Weakley, Clare G. II. Title. III. Series:
Wesley, John, 1703–1791. Wesley library for today's readers.
BX8333.W418N37   1988   234'.8   87–34111
ISBN 1–55661–013–0 (pbk.)

Dedication

This book is dedicated to
Jessica, Pam, and Sonny
with prayers for their continuing
blessings through the grace of
our Lord and Savior Jesus Christ

The Wesley Library for Today's Reader

JOHN WESLEY (1703–1791) was the founder of Methodism. Although raised in a godly home and trained for the ministry at Oxford, Wesley's failure as a missionary to the colonists and Indians in Georgia (1735–1738) revealed his unsaved condition. Strongly influenced upon his return to England by the Moravian, Peter Böhler, Wesley was converted (May 1738) to genuine faith in Christ while reading Luther's preface to Romans.

Shortly after his conversion, Wesley visited the Moravian settlement at Herrnhut and met Count Zinzendorf. He returned to England and embarked on his lifework. His objective was "to reform the nation, particularly the Church, and to spread Scriptural holiness over the land." He declared that he had only "one point of view—to promote so far as I am able, vital, practical religion; and by the grace of God to beget, preserve, and increase the life of God in the souls of men." Some have viewed him as the eighteenth-century apostle commissioned to evangelize Great Britain.

Wesley discovered the most effective medium for reaching the masses was open-air preaching, and his life became one of an itinerant preacher. Facing the Church's resistance to his evangelical doctrine, Wesley formed societies in the wake of his mission. The organization of Methodism was thus a direct outcome of his success in preaching the gospel. Wesley's writings include his now classic *Journals*, sermons, letters, expositions, tracts, histories, and abridgments.

CLARE WEAKLEY, JR. is a businessman, lecturer, and chaplain-at-large in his community. He received a B.B.A. and a M.Th. from Southern Methodist University. He is married and he and his family make their home in Dallas.

Preface

Gladly accept today whatever God permits this day to come upon you. Do not look upon the problems of tomorrow. "Sufficient unto the day is the evil thereof." Evil it is, speaking in the manner of men, whether it be reproach, or want, or pain, or sickness. But, in the language of God, all is a blessing. It is a precious balm prepared by the wisdom of God and variously dispensed among His children, according to the various needs of their souls. And He gives in one day sufficient for that day, proportioned to the need and strength of the person. If you snatch today what belongs to tomorrow, if you add this to what is given to you already, it will be more than you can bear. This is the way not to heal but to destroy your own soul. Therefore, take just as much as He gives you today. Today, do and accept His will. Today, give up yourself—your body, soul, and spirit—to God through Jesus. Desire nothing but that God may be glorified in all that you are, all you do, and all that you suffer. Seek nothing but to know God and His Son Jesus through the eternal Holy Spirit. Pursue nothing other than to love Him, to serve Him, and to enjoy Him in this hour and all eternity.

John Wesley
"Upon Our Lord's Sermon on The Mount," Sermon XXIX, Discourse IX, paragraph 29

Contents

Introduction

From his earliest introduction to the "new living faith" by Peter Böhler, John Wesley understood holiness and happiness to be irrevocably linked together. His journal entry of March 23, 1738, testifies: "I met Peter Böhler again, who now amazed me more and more by the account he gave of the fruits of living faith—the holiness and happiness which he affirmed to attend it."

After Wesley's rebirth at Aldersgate Street, he began his new pilgrimage with the Spirit, which tested this theology in the best and worst situations of his life. He never deviated from his initial conviction of its truth.

Wesley based all of his ministry on his personal rebirth experience and the conviction holiness was both necessary and achievable in this life. So we see both points in the sermons of this book. We must be born again in order to achieve the perfection demanded by God. Those lacking the rebirth will neither understand nor desire holiness. It is from this experience, which brings the indwelling Holy Spirit, that one then desires and is empowered to "work out his salvation with fear and trembling," living the holy life.

As Wesley pondered the need for holiness and worked toward it in his long life and ministry, he preached and wrote of experiences from a scriptural basis. Fourteen of his sermons are collected in this fifth book, *The Nature of Holiness*, in the series The Wesley Library for Today's Reader. Wesley's sermons were selected and grouped under the theme, *The Nature of Holiness,* because they seemed to present a basic starting point for those meditating on essentials of the Christian faith.

In this group of sermons, we find Wesley's understanding of man's predicament and a survey of many of his limitations. Next follows the need for God and faith in Him. Later come sermons on the problems that keep man from a complete commitment to Him. In all his sermons Wesley encourages us to keep up the good fight and to go on toward perfection. From beginning to end he affirms God's love and the free grace He gives through Jesus Christ to reconcile all of us to Him.

The bedrock of all this is Wesley's tried and tested belief that, as Juvenal wrote, *nemo malus felix* (no wicked man is happy). "All the general sources of sin—pride, self-will, and idolatry—are, in the same proportion as they prevail, general sources of misery. Therefore, as long as they reign in the soul, happiness cannot come in there. But they must reign until our basic nature is changed; that is, until we are born again. Consequently, the new birth is absolutely necessary in order to have happiness in this world, as well as the world to come."*

Wesley's sermons always invite all who will listen to try and test his new living faith, a faith not of human knowledge but of a supernatural work in the heart. That faith enters into the heart and changes the life and mind. It replaces unhappy inward feelings, attitudes, and emotions with happy ones. These new happy emotions produce a "joy unspeakable," along with peace, joy, and righteousness—heaven on earth.

This is an experiential faith that can be experienced, and

---

*John Wesley, "The New Birth," *Forty-four Sermons* (London: The Epworth Press, 1944), Sermon XXXIX, Vol. 3, p. 3).

proven, by everyone. With the Spirit as the power and Jesus as the guide, each can enter into the kingdom of heaven and experience holiness in this life.

John Wesley experienced this grace in his life and challenges, exhorts, and encourages each of us to "seek, ask, and knock" for the same righteousness.

Clare G. Weakley, Jr.
Dallas, Texas
September 1, 1987

1

The Imperfections of Human Knowledge

We know in part. (1 Corinthians 13:9)

The hunger for knowledge is a universal desire in man, fixed in the inner nature. It is constant in everyone, unless suspended by some stronger desire. It is insatiable, and is implanted in every human soul for God's purposes. This desire is intended to keep us from being content in anything here below, to raise our thoughts higher and higher, until we ascend to the source of all knowledge and all excellence, our wise and loving Creator.

Although our desire for knowledge has no bounds, our knowledge has. It is confined within very narrow bounds, much more narrow than people imagine, or the educated are willing to admit. There is a strong intimation, since God does nothing in vain, that in some future state of being our now insatiable desire will be satisfied, and there will be no longer the distance between the desire and the satisfaction.

Man's present knowledge is exactly adapted to his

Taken from John Wesley's, *Sermons on Several Occasions*, "The Imperfection of Human Knowledge," (New York: Carlton & Porter, 1857) LXXIV, Vol. 2, p. 116 ff.

present wants. It is sufficient to warn us of, and to preserve us from, most of the dangers to which we are now exposed, and to give us whatever is necessary for us as babes in Christ. We know enough of the nature and qualities of the things around us, so far as they relate to the health and strength of our bodies. We know how to procure and prepare our food. We know what clothing is fit to cover us. We know how to build our houses and to furnish them with all necessities and conveniences. We know just as much as is conducive to our living comfortably in this world. However, of many things above, below, and around us, we know little more than that they exist. In this deep ignorance we see the goodness as well as the wisdom of God, in His cutting short our knowledge on every side, purposefully to strip away our pride.

It is by their very nature that the wisest of men know but in part. How amazingly small a part do they know, either of the Creator or of His works. This is a very necessary but unpleasant theme, for vain man wants to be wise. Let us reflect upon this a bit. May the God of wisdom and love open our eyes to discern our own ignorance.

Our Limited Knowledge of God

Begin with the great Creator himself. How astonishingly little we know about God. How small a part of His nature or His essential attributes do we know. What conception can we form of His omnipresence? Who is able to comprehend how God is in this and every place and how He fills the immensity of space? If early philosophers, by denying the existence of a vacuum, only meant that there is no place empty of God, that every point of infinite space is full of God, certainly no man could question them. But still, what is omnipresence? Man is no more able to comprehend this than to understand the universe.

Sir Isaac Newton illustrated the omnipresence, or immensity, of God by terming infinite space the brain of the

Deity. Even heathens say, "All things are full of God." God himself said, "Do not I fill heaven and earth?" How beautifully the psalmist illustrates this. "Whither shall I go from thy spirit? or whither shall I flee from thy presence? If I ascend up into heaven, thou art there: if I make my bed in hell, behold, thou art there. If I take the wings of the morning, and dwell in the uttermost parts of the sea; even there shall thy hand lead me, and thy right hand shall hold me" (Ps. 139:7–10).

But in the meantime, what conception do we have either of His eternity or immensity? Such knowledge is too wonderful for us. We cannot grasp it.

A second essential attribute of God is eternity. He existed before all time. Perhaps we might more properly say, He exists from everlasting to everlasting. But what is eternity? One said that the divine eternity is "the at once entire and perfect possession of never ending life." But how much wiser are we for this definition? We know just as much from it as we did before. "The at once entire and perfect possession"— who understands what this means?

If indeed God had stamped, as some believe, an idea of himself on every human soul, we must certainly have understood something of these as well as His other attributes. We cannot suppose He would have impressed upon us either a false or an imperfect idea of himself. But the truth is, no man ever did, nor does now, find any such idea stamped upon his soul. The little we do know of God, except what we receive by the inspiration of the Holy Spirit, we do not gather from any inward impression but gradually acquire from without. The invisible things of God, if they are known at all, are known from the things that are made, from what He has written in all His works, not from what He has written in our hearts.

Our Limited Knowledge of Creation

So then, from His works, particularly His works of creation, we learn the knowledge of God. But it is not easy to see how little we know even of these. Begin with those that are at a distance. Who knows how far the universe extends? What are its limits? This is utterly hidden. And what do we know of the stars? Who knows the number of them, even that small portion we call the Milky Way? And who knows this function? Are they so many suns that illuminate their respective planets? Or do they minister only to this one, and contribute in some unknown way to the perpetual circulation of light and spirit? Who knows what comets are? Are they planets not fully formed or planets destroyed by fire? Or are they bodies of a wholly different nature, of which we have no idea? Who can tell what the sun is? Its use we know, but who knows how it came alive? We are not yet able to determine its true nature. We know the precise distance of our sun from the earth, but how many suns exist? After all, we know little of the universe. We have only uncertain conjectures concerning the nearest of all the planets.

Let us focus on things that are still nearer home, and ask what knowledge we have of them. How much do we know of that wonderful body "light"? How is it given to us? Does it flow in a continual stream from the sun, or does the sun impel the particles next to its orb, and so on and on, to the extremity of its system? And, does light gravitate or not? Does it attract or repel other bodies? Is it subject to the general laws that appear in all other matter, or is it a body altogether different from all other matter? Who can explain the phenomena of electricity? Who knows why some bodies superconduct and others do not? A thousand more questions are still being asked, which no man living can answer.

Now consider the earth on which we tread, and which God has peculiarly given to us. Do we understand this? Suppose our planet is properly measured. How much more of this do we know? Who can inform us what lies beneath its crust, the region of stones, metals, minerals, and other fossils? This is only a thin layer, which is a very small proportion of the whole. Who can teach us the inner parts of the globe? Is there a central fire, a grand reservoir, which not only supplies the volcanoes, but also ministers to the ripening of gems and metals, and perhaps to the production of vegetables and the well-being of animals, too? Or is a great, deep, central abyss of waters still contained in the bowels of the earth? Who has seen and who can tell? Who can give any solid satisfaction to a rational inquirer?

How much of the very surface of the globe is still utterly unknown to us. How very little we know of the polar regions, both north and south, how little of those vast countries, the inland parts either of Africa or South America. Much less do we know what is contained in the great oceans that cover so large a part of the globe. Most of its chambers are inaccessible to man, so that we cannot tell how they are furnished. How little we know of those things on the dry land that fall directly under our notice. Consider even the most simple metals or stones. How imperfectly we know their complete nature and properties. There is still mystery in even the most common of elements.

With regard to animals, are microscopic animals real animals? If they are, are they not essentially different from all other animals in the universe, as not requiring any food, not generating or being generated? How totally ignorant are the most knowledgeable of men regarding the whole affair of generation, even the generation of men.

In the book of the Creator, indeed, were all our members written, which were fashioned when as yet there were none of them. But by what rule were they fashioned, and in what manner? By what means was the first motion communicated? When, and how, was the immortal spirit added to the senseless clay? It is mystery and we can only say, "I am fearfully and wonderfully made" (Ps. 139:14). Many discoveries regarding insects have been made recently. But how little is all that is discovered in comparison to what is undiscovered. How many millions of them, by their extreme minuteness, totally escape all our attention? And, indeed, even the minute parts of the largest animals elude our scrutiny. Do we have a more complete knowledge of fish than we have of insects? A great part, if not the greatest part, of the inhabitants of the waters are totally concealed from us. It is probable the species of sea animals are as numerous as the land animals, but how few are known to us. And how little we know of those few. With birds we are a little better acquainted, and it is but a little, for of very many we know hardly any more than their outward shape. We know a few of the obvious properties of others, chiefly those that frequent our houses. But we have not a thorough, adequate knowledge even of them. We do not know how different qualities arise in different species, or in individuals of the same species, and frequently in those that come from the same parents. Are they mere machines? What can they know or remember?

Our Limited Knowledge of Ourselves

Let us consider man. Do we know ourselves, our bodies, and our souls? What is our soul? It is a spirit, we know. But what is a spirit? Here we are at a full stop. And where is the soul lodged? In the pineal gland? In the brain? In the heart? In the blood? In any single part of the body? Or, if anyone can understand those terms, all in all, and all in every part? How is the soul united to the body? A spirit to a clod? What is the secret, imperceptible chain that couples them together? Can the wisest of men give a satisfactory answer to any one of these plain questions? As to our body itself, how little we know. A night's sleep is less for some than for others. Who can account for this? What is flesh? That of the muscles in particular? Are the fibers that compose it of a determinate size? How does a muscle act? By being contracted and consequently shortened? But how is it contracted? If with nerves, how and from where does the stimuli come? And where does it go the moment the muscle is relaxed? Are the nerves permeable or solid? How do they act? What is sleep? Of what does it consist? What is dreaming? How can we know dreams from waking thoughts? No man knows.

Seeing how little we do know, even about ourselves, what

can we expect to know about the whole creation of God? Are we not better acquainted with His works of providence than with His works of creation?

God's Unsearchable Ways

One of the first principles of religion is that His kingdom rules over all. So we say with confidence, "Oh, Lord our Lord, how excellent is thy name in all the earth!" (Ps. 8:1). It is a childish conceit to suppose chance governs the world, or has any part in the government of it, even in those things that appear to be perfectly casual. "The lot is cast into the lap; but the whole disposing thereof is from the Lord" (Prov. 16:33). Our blessed Jesus himself has put this matter beyond all possible doubt. Not a sparrow, said He, falls to the ground without the will of your Father who is in heaven. He expressed the thing more strongly still, saying, "The very hairs of your head are all numbered" (Matt. 10:30).

Although we are well aware of this general truth, that all things are governed by the providence of God, yet how amazingly little we know of the particulars contained in this belief. How little we understand of His providential dealings with regard to nations, families, and individuals. There are heights and depths in all these that our understanding can in no way fathom. We comprehend but a small part of His ways now, and the rest we shall know only in the hereafter. With regard to entire nations, how little we understand of God's providential dealings with them. Innumerable nations in the Eastern world once flourished, to the terror of all those around them, and are now swept away from the face of the earth. Their memorials have perished with them. Nor has the case been any different in the West. In Europe we know of many large and powerful kingdoms, of which only the names are left. Their people have vanished as if they had never been. But why it has pleased Almighty God to sweep them away with the broom of destruction, we do not know. This is especially mysterious because those who succeeded them often were little better than their predecessors.

But it is not only with regard to ancient nations that the providential dispensations of God are utterly incomprehensible to us. The same difficulties occur now. We cannot account for His present dealings with the inhabitants of the earth. We know "the Lord is good to all: and his tender mercies are over all his works" (Ps. 145:9). But we do not know how to reconcile this with the present dispensations of His providence. At this moment, is not almost every part of the earth full of ignorance, evil, and cruelty? In what a condition, in particular, is the large and populous India? How many hundred thousands of the poor, quiet people have been destroyed and their carcasses left as garbage? In what a condition, though they have no Western ruffians there, are numberless people in the Far East? How little is their state above that of animals. And who cares either for their souls or their bodies? But the Father of all men cares for them. Oh, mystery of Providence.

And who cares for thousands, if not millions, of wretched Africans? Who cares that they are outcasts of men? Oh, Father of mercies, these are the works of your own hands, the purchase of your Son's blood.

How little better is either the civil or religious state of the poor American Indians, that is, the miserable remains of them. In some places, not one of them is left alive. In the Caribbean, when the "Christians" first came, there were three million inhabitants. Scarcely twelve thousand of them survived the Spanish. And in what condition are these, or the other Indians who are still scattered up and down the continents of South or North America? Few have any Christianity or public worship of any kind. God is not in all their thoughts. Most of them have no modern civil government at all. Every man does what is right in his own eyes. Therefore, they are decreasing daily, and very probably, in a century or two, there will not be one of them left.

The inhabitants of Europe are not in quite so deplorable a condition. They are in a state of civilization. They have useful laws and are governed by magistrates. They have religion and claim they are Christians. But whether they are called Christians or not, many of them have not much religion. What do you say to thousands who live in high northern latitudes? Are they as civilized? Add to these, myriads of humans who are freezing among the snows of Siberia and as many, if not more, who are wandering up and down in the deserts of Tartary. Add thousands upon thousands of Muslims and so-called Christians from the Middle East. God did so love these that He gave His Son, His only begotten Son, to the end they might not perish, but have everlasting life!

Then, why are they so? Oh, wonder above all wonders. There is something equally mysterious in the divine dispensation with regard to Christianity itself. Why is Christianity not spread as far as sin? Why is this Medicine not sent to every place where the disease is found? Alas, it is not. The sound of it has not gone forth into all lands. Poison is diffused over the whole globe, but the true antidote is not known in a sixth part of it. How is it that the wisdom and goodness of God allows the true antidote itself to be so grievously adulterated, not only in Roman Catholic countries, but almost in every part of the Christian world? It is so adulterated, by mixing it frequently with useless, frequently with poisonous ingredients, that it retains none, or at least only a very small part of its original virtue. It is so thoroughly adulterated by many of those very persons whom He has sent to administer it that it adds tenfold malignity to the disease it was designed to cure. In consequence of this, there is little more mercy or truth to be found among "Christians" than among pagans.

It has been claimed that many so-called Christians are far worse than the heathen who surround them, being more profligate and more abandoned to all manner of wickedness, neither fearing God nor regarding man. Who can comprehend this? Does not He who is higher than the highest consider it? Equally incomprehensible to us are many of the divine dispensations regarding particular families. We cannot understand why He raises some to wealth, honor, and power, but depresses others with poverty and various afflictions. Some prosper wonderfully in all they attempt, and the world pours in upon them. Others, with all their labor and toil, can scarcely procure daily bread. Often prosperity and applause continue with the former to their death, yet the latter drink the cup of adversity to their life's end. We can find no reason either for the prosperity of one or the adversity of the other.

Neither can we account for the divine dispensations regarding individuals. We do not know why the lot of this man is cast in Europe, and the lot of that man in the wilds of Africa. Neither why one is born rich or noble, while the other is of poor parents. Nor do we know why the father and mother of one are strong and healthy, yet those of another weak and diseased consequently becoming a miserable being all the days of his life, exposed to want, and pain, and a thousand temptations, from which he finds no escape. How many are, from their very infancy, hedged in with such relations that they seem to have no chance, no possibility of being useful to themselves or others? Why are they, outside their own choice, entangled in such connections? Why are harmful people so cast in their way that they don't know how to escape? Why are useful persons hidden from their sight, or snatched away from them at these floundering individuals' utmost need? Oh, God, how unsearchable are your counsels, too deep to be fathomed by our reason, and your ways of executing those counsels are far beyond our wisdom.

Are we able to search out His works of grace any more than His works of providence? Nothing is more sure than that without holiness no man shall see the Lord (Heb. 12:14). Why is it, then, that so vast a majority of mankind are, so far as we can judge, cut off from all possibility of holiness, even from their mother's womb? For instance, what possibility is there that an inhabitant of a nonreligious place, if he lives and dies there, should ever know what holiness means, or, consequently, ever attain it? Heathens may say, "He sinned before he was born, in a pre-existent state. Therefore, he was placed here in such an unfavorable situation that through mercy he should have a second trial."

Supposing there was such a pre-existent state. This, which you call a second trial, is really no trial at all, because as soon as that heathen is born into the world, he is in the powerful grip of his savage parents and relations, who, from the first dawn of reason, train him up in their same ignorance, atheism, and barbarity. He has no chance, so to speak; he has no possibility of any better education. What trial has he then? From the time he comes into the world until he goes out of it again, he seems to be under a dire necessity of living in all ungodliness and unrighteousness. How can this be the case with so many millions of the souls that God has made? Is not God the God of all the ends of the earth and of them that remain in the broad sea?

It may be observed that if this conjecture is extended into an objection against revelation, it is an objection that lies against natural, as well as revealed, religion. If the objection were conclusive, it would not drive us into deism, but into flat atheism. It would argue not only against the Christian revelation but against there being a God. Yet I do not see how we can avoid the force of it except by resolving all into the unsearchable wisdom of God, along with a deep conviction of our own ignorance and inability to fathom His counsels.

Even among us, who are favored far above these, to whom are entrusted the truths of God, whose Word is a lantern to our feet and a light in all our paths, there are still many circumstances in His dispensations that are far above our understanding. We do not know why He allowed us to go on in our own ways so long before we were convinced of sin, or why He made use of this or that instrument, in this or that manner. There are a thousand circumstances attending the process of our conviction that we do not understand. We do not know why He allowed us to wait so long, before He revealed His Son in our hearts, or why our change from darkness to light was accompanied with its particular circumstances. It is doubtless the peculiar right of God to reserve the times and seasons in His own power. And we cannot give any reason why, of two persons equally thirsting for salvation, one is presently taken into the favor of God, and the other left to yearn for months or years. One, as soon as he calls upon God, is answered and filled with peace and joy in believing, yet another seeks after Him, and, it seems, with the same degree of sincerity and earnestness, and still cannot find Him or any consciousness of His favor, for weeks, or months, or years. We know well this cannot possibly be due to any absolute decree, consigning one, before he was born, to everlasting glory, and the other to everlasting fire, but we do not know the reason for it. Only God knows that.

Likewise, there is great variety in the manner and time of God's bestowing His sanctifying grace, whereby He enables His children to give Him their whole heart. We can in no way account for this. We do not know why He bestows this on some, even before they ask for it—some unquestionable instances of which we have seen—and on some, after they had sought it but a few days. Yet He permits other believers to wait for it, perhaps twenty, thirty, or forty years, and even others until a few hours or even minutes before their death.

For the various circumstances also that attend the fulfilling of that great promise, "The Lord thy God will circumcise thine heart . . . to love the Lord thy God, with all thine heart, and with all thy soul," God undoubtedly has reasons. But those reasons are generally hidden from the children of men. Here some of those who are enabled to love God with all their heart, and with all their soul, retain the same blessing without any interruption, till they are carried off to Abraham's bosom. Others do not retain this first love, although they are not conscious of having grieved the Holy Spirit of God. This also we do not understand. We do not know the mind of the Spirit.

Several valuable lessons may be learned from a deep consciousness of our own ignorance. First, we may learn a lesson of humility and not think of ourselves, particularly with regard to our understanding, more highly than we ought to think. We must become thoroughly convinced that we are not sufficient in ourselves to think one good thought. We would stumble at every step, and err every moment of our lives, were it not that we have an anointing from the Holy One, who abides with us. Were it not that He who knows what is in man helps our infirmities, and that there is a Spirit in man which gives wisdom, inspiration, and understanding, we would be totally lacking. From this we may also learn a lesson of faith and confidence in God. A full conviction of our own ignorance should teach us full trust in His wisdom. It may teach us that which is not always so easy as one would think: to trust the invisible God a bit further than we can see Him. It may assist us in learning that difficult lesson, to cast down our own imaginations—or reasonings, as the word properly signifies—to cast down everything that exalts itself against the knowledge of God, and bring into captivity every thought to the obedience of Christ (2 Cor. 10:5).

There are, at present, two grand obstructions to our forming a right judgment about God's dealings with men. The one is, there are innumerable facts relating to every man, which we do not and cannot know. Those facts are, at present, hidden from us, and covered from our search by impenetrable darkness. The other is, we cannot see the thoughts of men, even when we see their actions. Moreover, we do not know their intentions, and without this, we can but poorly judge their outward action. Be conscious of this and judge nothing concerning His providential dispensations until He brings to light the hidden things of darkness and manifests the thoughts and intents of the heart.

From a consciousness of our ignorance we may learn, finally, a lesson of resignation. We may be led to say, at all times, and in all instances, "Father, not as I will; but as thou wilt." This was the last lesson that our blessed Jesus, as a man, learned while He was upon earth. He could go no higher than, "Not as I will, but as thou wilt," until He bowed His head and gave up the ghost. Let us also be made conformable to His death, so we may know the full power of His resurrection!

2

Reason Impartially Considered

Brethren, be not children in understanding: howbeit in malice be ye children, but in understanding be men. (1 Corinthians 14:20)

A famous man who had made many observations on human nature once remarked, "If reason be against a man, a man will always be against reason." This fact has been confirmed by the experience of all ages. From the earliest times, there have been many instances of it in the Christian as well as the heathen world. Even then there were many well-meaning people who, not having much reason themselves, imagined that reason was of no use in religion; rather, it was a hindrance. Unfortunately, there has been a great succession of men who have believed and declared the same thing. Never was there a greater number of these in the Christian Church than at this day.

Among those who despise and belittle reason are fanatics who suppose the dreams of their own imagination to be revelations from God. We cannot expect them to have much regard for reason. Having themselves as an infallible guide, they are little moved by the reasonings of others. Foremost

Taken from John Wesley's, *Sermons on Several Occasions*, "The Case of Reason Impartially Considered," LXXV, Vol. 2, p. 126 ff.

of these are the Antinomians; for however they may differ in other respects, they agree in making void the law through faith. If you oppose them, when they are asserting propositions full of absurdity and blasphemy, they will probably think it sufficient to answer, "Oh, that is your carnal reasoning." Therefore, all arguments are lost upon them. They regard your assertions as no more than stubble.

How natural it is for those who witness one extreme to go too far the other way. While they strongly oppose absurd and undervalued reason, they are apt to overvalue it. It is much easier for many to run from one extreme to another than to stop in the middle. Accordingly, we are surrounded by those who propose, as an undoubted principle, reason as the highest gift of God. Men of this persuasion paint it in the fairest colors, extolling it to the skies. They are fond of exalting in its praise. They make reason little less than divine, and are apt to describe it as very nearly, if not quite, infallible. They look upon it as the all-sufficient director of all people, able by its native light to guide them into all truth and lead them into all virtue.

They who are prejudiced against Christianity and do not believe the Scriptures as the Word of God almost universally run into this extreme. I have rarely known any exception. So do those, no matter what they are called, who deny the divinity of Christ. Indeed, some of these say they do not deny His Godhead, only His supreme Godhead. But that is the same thing, for in denying Him to be the supreme God, they deny Him to be any God at all, unless they claim there are two gods, a great one and a little one.

All these are outspoken defenders of reason as the great unerring guide. To these overvaluers of reason we may generally add men of eminently strong understanding, who, because they do know more than most other men, suppose they can know all things. But we may also add many who are at the other extreme—men of eminently weak understanding, men in whom pride takes the place of sense. They do not know they are blind because they have always been blind.

Is there, then, no medium between these extremes, undervaluing and overvaluing reason? Certainly there is. But who can mark the middle way? I will cautiously try to supply this great defect by pointing out, first to the undervaluers what reason can do, and then to the overvaluers what reason cannot do.

But before we proceed it is absolutely necessary to define reason and know the precise meaning of the word. Unless this is done, men may dispute for eternity without coming to any concrete conclusion. Not knowing the correct definition of reason causes many arguments on the subject. Very few disputants thought of defining the word they were disputing about. Consequently, they were just as far from agreement at the end as at the beginning. "Reason" is sometimes used for "argument," as in "Give me a reason for your statement," or, in Isaiah, "Bring forth your strong reasons." We use the word in nearly the same sense when we say, "He has good reasons for what he does." It seems here to mean, he has sufficient motives to influence a wise man.

But how is the word to be understood concerning the "reasons of things," particularly when it is asked whether the reasons of things are eternal? Do not the "reasons of things" here mean the "relations" of things to each other? But what are the eternal relations of earthly things, of things which did not exist until yesterday? Could the relations of these things exist before the things themselves had any existence? Is not that a flat contradiction?

In another use of the word, reason is much the same as "understanding." It means a faculty of the human soul, which exerts itself in three ways: by simple knowledge, judgment, and discourse. *Simple knowledge* is barely conceiving a thing in the mind, the first and most simple act of understanding; *judgment* is determining that the things before known either agree with, or differ from, one another; *discourse*, strictly speaking, is the motion or progress of the mind, from one judgment to another. The faculty of the soul that includes these three operations is what I mean by the term reason. Taking the word in this sense, let us now impartially consider what reason can do.

The Benefits of Reason

Who can deny that reason can do much in the affairs of common life? It can direct employees as they perform their various duties at work. It can direct the farmer as he decides when to cultivate his ground, or when to plow, sow, reap, or bring in his corn. Reason will help him as he breeds and manages his cattle, and act with prudence and propriety in every part of his job. It can direct designers as they prepare various sorts of apparel, and a thousand necessities and conveniences of life, not only for themselves and their households, but for their neighbors, near and far. It can direct those of higher abilities to plan and execute works of a more elegant kind. It can direct the painter, the sculptor, and the musician to excel in their callings. It can direct the mariner to steer his course over the great deeps. It enables those who study the laws of their country to defend the property or life of their fellow citizens, and those who study the art of healing to cure most of the illnesses to which we are exposed in our present state.

On a higher scale, reason can assist us in going through the whole circle of arts and sciences, of grammar, rhetoric, logic, natural and moral philosophy, mathematics, algebra, and metaphysics. It can teach whatever skill or industry man has invented. It is absolutely necessary for the due discharge of the most important offices, such as magistrates, whether of an inferior or superior rank; and of subordinate or supreme governors, whether of states, provinces, or kingdoms. All this, few will deny. No thinking person can doubt that reason is of considerable value in all things relating to the present world.

But suppose we speak of higher things, the things of another world. What can reason do here? Is it a help or a hindrance to religion? What can it do in the things of God? It can do much, both with regard to its foundation and its superstructure. The foundation of true religion stands upon the oracles of God. It is built upon the prophets and apostles, Jesus Christ himself being the chief cornerstone. Now, of what excellent use is reason if we are to understand ourselves or explain to others those living oracles? How is it possible, without reason, to understand the essential truths contained therein, which are beautifully summarized in the Apostles' Creed? It is reason, assisted by the Holy Spirit, that enables us to understand what the Holy Scriptures declare concerning the being and attributes of God—His eternity and immensity, His power, wisdom and holiness.

It is by reason that God enables us, in some measure, to comprehend His method of dealing with us, and the nature of His various dispensations of the old and new covenants— the Law and Gospel. It is by His Spirit we understand what repentance is, what that faith is by which we are saved, what is the nature and condition of justification, what are the immediate and the subsequent fruits of it. By reason we learn what the new birth is, without which we cannot enter into the kingdom of heaven, and what holiness is, without which no man shall see the Lord.

By the due use of reason, we come to know the conditions implied in inward holiness, and what it is to be outwardly holy, holy in all manner of life. In other words, what is the mind of Christ, and what is it to walk as He walked. Many times we will need reason in order to keep a clear conscience. Often conscience cannot be understood without the exercise of our reason. The same is needed in order to understand and to discharge the ordinary duties of parents and children, of husbands and wives, and employers and employees.

In all these respects, and in all the duties of common life, God has given us our reason for a guide. It is only by acting on the principles of reason and by using all the understanding that God has given us that we can have a clear conscience toward God and man.

Here, then, is a large field indeed, wherein reason may extol and exercise all its powers. And if reason can do all this, both in civil and religious things, what is it that it cannot do?

The Shortcomings of Reason

First, reason cannot produce faith. Although faith is always consistent with reason, yet reason cannot produce faith in the scriptural sense of the word. Faith, according to Scripture, is an evidence, or conviction, of things not seen. It is a divine evidence, bringing a full conviction of an invisible, eternal world. It is true there was a kind of shadowy persuasion of this fact, even among some of the wiser heathens, probably from tradition or from some gleams of light reflected from the Israelites. Hence, many hundred years before our Lord was born, the Greek poet uttered that great truth: "Millions of spiritual creatures walk the earth unseen, whether we wake, or whether we sleep." But this was little more than faint conjecture. It was far from a firm conviction, which reason, in its highest state of improvement, could never produce in any child of man.

Many years ago, I found the truth of this by personal experience. I carefully heaped up the strongest arguments I could find, either in ancient or modern authors, to prove the existence of God, and, what is nearly connected with it, the existence of an invisible world. I wandered up and down, musing to myself, "What if all these things that I see around me, this earth and heaven, this universal frame, has existed from eternity? What if the melancholy supposition of the old poet is the real case? What if the generation of men is exactly parallel with the generation of leaves, if the earth drops its successive inhabitants just as the tree drops its leaves? What if that saying is really true, 'Death is nothing, and nothing is after death'? How am I to be sure that this is not the case, that I have not followed cunningly devised fables?" I pursued the thought until there was no spirit in me, and I was ready to choose death rather than life.

In a point of such unspeakable importance, do not depend on your reason or the word of another. Retire for a while from the busy world, and make the experiment yourself. See whether your reason will give you a clear, satisfactory evidence of the invisible world. After the prejudices of education are laid aside, produce your strong reasons for its existence. Set them all in array, silence all objections, and put all your doubts to flight. Alas, you cannot, with all your understanding. You may repress your doubts for a season, but how quickly will they rally again and attack you with redoubled violence. And what can poor reason do for your deliverance? The more vehemently you struggle, the more deeply you are entangled in the toils, and you find no way to escape. Such was the case with that great admirer of reason, the author of the maxim above cited, the philosopher, Thomas Hobbes. None will deny that he had a strong understanding. But did it produce in him a full and satisfactory conviction of an invisible world? Did it open the eyes of his understanding to see beyond the bounds of this earth? Far from it. His dying words ought never to be forgotten. "Where are you going, sir?" said one of his friends. He answered, "I am taking a leap in the dark!" and died. That is all the evidence of the invisible world bare reason can give to the wisest of men. Reason alone cannot produce scriptural hope in any child of man, whereby we rejoice in hope of the glory of God. That hope that the Bible in one place terms "tasting the powers of the world to come" (Heb. 6:5), in another, "sitting in heavenly places in Christ Jesus" (Eph. 2:6). That which enables us to say, "Blessed be the God and Father of our Lord Jesus Christ . . . [who] hath begotten us again unto a lively hope . . . to an inheritance incorruptible, and undefiled, and that fadeth not away, reserved in heaven" (1 Pet. 1:3–4). This hope can spring only from Christian faith; therefore, where there is no faith, there is no hope. Consequently, reason, being unable to produce faith, must be equally unable to produce hope.

Experience confirms this also. How often have I labored with all my might to generate this hope in myself. But it was lost labor. I could no more acquire this hope of heaven than I could touch heaven with my hand. And whoever of you makes the same attempt will find the same success. I do not deny that a self-deceiving fanatic may work in himself a kind of hope. He may work himself up into a lively imagination, into a sort of pleasing dream. He may even compass himself about with sparks of his own kindling, but this cannot be of long duration. In a little while the bubble will surely break. And what will follow? "This shall ye have of mine hand; ye shall lie down in sorrow" (Isa. 50:11).

If reason could have produced a hope of immortality in any person, it might have produced it in that great man Socrates, whom Justin Martyr called "a Christian before Christ." In what other heathen can we find so strong an understanding, joined with such consummate virtue? But had he really this hope? Let him answer for himself. What is the conclusion of that noble apology he made before his unrighteous judges? "And now, oh judges! ye are going hence to live; and I am going hence to die: which of these is best, the gods know; but, I suppose, no man does." No man knows! How far is this from the language of Paul, the little Benjamite, who wanted "to depart, and to be with Christ; which is far better" (Phil. 1:23). And how many thousands are there at this day, even in our own nation, young men and women, old men and children, who are able to witness the same good confession?

But who is able to do this by the force of reason, no matter how highly developed? One of the most sensible and amiable heathens who has lived since our Lord died was the Roman emperor Adrian. He said, "A prince ought to resemble the sun. He ought to shine on every part of his dominion, and to diffuse his salutary rays in every place where he comes." Adrian's life was a comment upon his word. Wherever he went, he executed justice and showed mercy. Was he not, then, at the close of a long life, full of immortal hope? We are able to answer this from his own pathetic dying words said to his own soul:

Poor, little, pretty, fluttering thing,
Must we no longer live together?
And dost thou prune thy trembling wing,
To take thy flight, thou know'st not whither?

Thy pleasing vein, thy humorous folly,
Lies all neglected, all forgot!
And pensive, wavering, melancholy,
Thou hop'st, and fear'st, thou know'st not what.

Reason, no matter how cultivated and improved, cannot produce the love of God. It cannot produce either faith or hope, from which alone this love can flow. It is only when we behold by faith the love the Father has bestowed upon us in giving us His only Son that we might not perish but have everlasting life, that the love of God is shed abroad in our hearts by the Holy Spirit. It is only then, when we rejoice in hope of the glory of God, that we love Him after He first loved us. What can cold reason do in this matter? It might present us with fair ideas. It can draw a fine picture of love, but that is only a painted fire. Reason cannot go any further than this. I made the trial for many years. I collected the finest hymns, prayers, and meditations I could find in any language. I said, sang, or read them over and over, with all possible seriousness and attention. Still I was like the bones in Ezekiel's vision—covered with skin, but having no life.

And as reason cannot produce the love of God, so neither can it produce the love of our neighbor—a calm, generous, unbiased benevolence to every child of man. This earnest, steady goodwill to our fellow creatures never flowed from any source but gratitude to our Creator. If this be the very essence of virtue, it follows that virtue can have no existence unless it springs from the love of God. Therefore, as reason cannot produce this love, so neither can it produce virtue.

And as it cannot give faith, hope, love, or virtue, so it cannot give happiness, since apart from these there can be no happiness for any intelligent creature. It is true, those who are void of all virtue may have pleasures, such as they are, but happiness they have not, nor can have. They may have pleasures, shadows, and dreams, but those are fleeting as the wind, and as unsubstantial as a rainbow. They are as unsatisfying to the poor grasping soul as the colors of an eastern cloud. None of these will stand the test of reflection. When thoughtful consideration comes, the bubble breaks.

Let me now add a few plain words, first to those who undervalue reason. Never more declaim in any wild, loose, ranting manner against God's precious gift of reason. Acknowledge this light of the Lord that He has put in our nature for excellent purposes. Note how many admirable questions it answers, even if only in the things of this life. Of what grand use is even a moderate share of reason in all our worldly employments, from the lowest offices of life through all the intermediate branches of business, until we ascend to those that are of the highest importance and the greatest difficulty?

When, therefore, you despise or depreciate reason, you must not imagine you are doing God a service. Least of all are you promoting the cause of God when you are endeavoring to exclude reason from religion. Unless you willfully shut your eyes, you cannot help but see of what service it is both in laying the foundation of true religion, under the guidance of the Spirit of God, and in raising the superstructure. Reason directs us in every point, both in faith and practice. It guides us with regard to every branch, both of inward and outward holiness. Do we not glory in this, that the whole of our religion is a reasonable service? Yes, and that every part of it, when it is duly performed, is the highest exercise of our understanding.

Now let us consider those who *overvalue* reason. Why should a person run from one extreme to the other? Is not the middle way best? *Let reason do all that reason can.* Use it as far as it will go. But, at the same time, acknowledge that reason is utterly incapable of giving faith, or hope, or love, and, consequently, of producing either real virtue or substantial happiness. Expect these from a higher source, the Father of all the world. Seek and receive these virtues, not as results of your own efforts but as gifts from God. Lift up your hearts to Him who gives to all men liberally, without finding fault. He alone can give that faith which is the evidence and conviction of things not seen. He alone can give you new birth, a living hope of an eternal inheritance in the heavens, and He alone can pour out this love in your heart by the Holy Spirit whom He has given to you. Therefore, ask and it shall be given to you. Cry out to Him, and you will not cry in vain. How can you doubt? "If ye then, being evil, know how to give good gifts unto your children: how much more shall your heavenly Father give the Holy Spirit to them that ask Him" (Luke 11:13)? Then you shall be living witnesses that wisdom, holiness, and happiness are one, inseparably united, and are, indeed, the beginning of that eternal life which God has given us in Jesus.

3

The Wisdom of God's Counsels

O the depth of the riches both of the wisdom and knowl-edge of God! (Romans 11:33)

Some understand that the wisdom and knowledge of God mean the same thing. Others believe that the wisdom of God more directly refers to His directing all things, while His knowledge is the means that He has prepared and made conducive to His ends. The first seems to be the most natural understanding, because the wisdom of God in its most extensive meaning must include the one as well as the other, the means as well as the ends.

Now the wisdom, as well as the power of God, is manifested in His creation and in the formation and arrangement of all His works. We see it in heaven above and in the earth beneath, and in adapting this to the various ends for which they were designed. So each of them, apart from the rest, is good, but together they are very good, harmonizing in one connected system for the happiness of His intelligent creatures and to His glory. This wisdom appears even to short-sighted men, but much more to spirits of a higher order. It is apparent in the creation, disposition and preservation of

Taken from John Wesley's, *Sermons on Several Occasions*, "The Wisdom of God's Counsels," LXXIII, Vol. 2, p. 108 ff.

the whole universe. He upholds all things by the word of His power.

His wisdom can also be seen in the permanent government of all that He has created. How admirably does His wisdom direct the heavenly bodies! Whether those are fixed or wander, they never leave their orbits. How well He superintends all the parts of this lower world, this speck of creation, the earth, so that all things are still as they were at the beginning. Beautiful in their seasons, summer and winter, seed time and harvest, they are always regular. Yes, all things serve their Creator. Fire and hail, snow and vapor, wind and storm, fulfill His word, so that we may well say, "O Lord our Lord, how excellent is thy name in all the earth!" (Ps. 8:1).

The wisdom of God can also be seen in the government of nations, states, and kingdoms, perhaps even more so here than in His inanimate creation—that is if we can make such a statement, that God's wisdom is more easily seen in one area than another. The whole inanimate creation, being totally passive and inert, can make no opposition to His will. Therefore, in the natural world, all things roll on in an even, uninterrupted course. But it is far different in the moral world. Here evil men and evil spirits continually oppose the divine will, and create innumerable irregularities. Here, therefore, is the perfect arena for the exercise of all the riches both of the wisdom and knowledge of God, in counteracting the wickedness of men, and the subtlety of Satan, in order to carry on His own glorious design, which is the salvation of lost mankind. Were He to do this by an absolute decree and by His own irresistible power, it would imply no wisdom at all. His wisdom is shown by saving man without destroying human nature or taking away personal liberty.

But the riches of the wisdom and knowledge of God are most obvious in His church. He planted His wisdom like a grain of mustard seed, the least of all seeds, and preserved and continually increased it until it grew into a great tree, overcoming the uninterrupted opposition of all the evil powers. Paul justly terms this the manifold wisdom of God. It is a uniquely expressive word, intimating that this wisdom, in the manner of its operation, is diversified a thousand ways. These things the highest angels seek to see, yet never fully comprehend. It seems to be with regard to these, chiefly, that Paul utters that strong exclamation, "How unsearchable are his judgments, and his ways past finding out!" (Rom. 11:33). The psalms agree that "his footsteps are not known" (Ps. 77:19).

But He has been pleased to reveal some of this to us. By keeping closely to what God has revealed, meantime comparing the word and the work of God together, we may understand a part of His ways. We may, in some measure, trace this wonderful wisdom from the beginning of the world, from Adam to Noah, from Noah to Moses, and from Moses to Jesus. But consider it only with regard to what He has done in our present age, and the more recent past.

In the fullness of time, when it seemed best in His wisdom, God brought His only begotten into the world. He then laid the foundation of His church, though it hardly appeared until the day of Pentecost. From then it was a glorious church; all the members thereof being filled with the Holy Spirit, with one heart and of one mind, continuing steadfastly in the apostles' doctrine, in fellowship, in the breaking of bread, and in prayers. In fellowship, they had all things in common, no man counting anything he had as his own.

This happy state did not continue long. Ananias and Sapphira, through the love of money, the root of all evil, made the first breach in the community of goods. Note the partiality, the unjust respect of persons on the one side, and resentment and murmuring on the other, even while the apostles themselves presided over the church at Jerusalem. See the grievous spots and wrinkles that were soon found in every part of the church, recorded not only in the Acts, but in the epistles of Paul, James, Peter, and John. A still fuller account is in John's Revelation. According to this, what a tragedy was the first-century Christian Church, even before

John died, if we may judge the state of the church in general from the state of the particular churches described in Revelation. From that time, for fourteen hundred years, it was corrupted more and more, as all history shows, till few if any had either the power or form of religion left.

Nevertheless, the gates of hell never did totally prevail against it. God always reserved a seed for himself, a few Christians who worshiped Him in spirit and in truth. I have often wondered if these were not the very persons labeled as heretics by the rich and honorable Christians, who will always have number as well as power on their side. Perhaps it was chiefly this wile of the devil and his demons that caused the good which was in them to be called evil, thereby preventing them from being as extensively useful as they otherwise might have been.

When iniquity had overspread Christendom as a flood, the Spirit of the Lord lifted up a standard against it. He raised up a poor monk, without wealth, without power, and, at that time, without friends, to declare war, as it were, against the bishop of Rome and all his adherents. Martin Luther, this little stone chosen of God, soon grew into a great mountain, and increased more and more. Yet even before Luther was called home, the faith of many waxed cold. Many who had once been faithful witnesses turned back from the holy commandment delivered to them. The greater part of those who once experienced the power of faith made shipwreck of it. Despair over this was thought to be the occasion of Luther's fatal illness. He uttered those melancholy words: "I have spent my strength for naught! Those who are called by my name, are, it is true, reformed in opinions and modes of worship, but in their hearts and lives, in their tempers and practice, they are not a jot better than the Papists!" Soon after, he died.

About the same time it pleased God to visit Great Britain. A few during the reign of Henry VIII, and many more in the three following reigns, became real witnesses of true, scriptural Christianity. The number of these greatly increased in the beginning of the following century. In the year 1627, there was a wonderful outpouring of the Spirit in several parts of England as well as in Scotland and the north of Ireland. But riches and honor poured in upon them as well, and their hearts began to be estranged from God and started cleaving to the present world. As soon as persecution ceased, the Christians who were once poor and despised became invested with power, ease, and affluence. Their change of circumstances brought a change of spirit. Riches and honor quickly produced the usual effects. Receiving the world, they quickly loved the world. They no longer panted after heaven, but became more and more attached to the material things of earth. After a few years, one who knew and loved them well, and was an exceptional judge of men and manners, deeply grieved over them for having lost all the life and power of religion, to become the same as those whom they had despised as trash in the streets.

The little religion that was left in the land received another deadly wound at the Restoration through one of the worst princes who ever sat on the English throne, along with the most abandoned court in Europe. Infidelity now broke in and overspread the land as a flood. Of course, all kind of immorality came with it, and increased to the end of that century. Some feeble attempts were made to stem the torrent during the reign of Queen Anne, but it still increased till about the year 1725, when William Law published his *Practical Treatise on Christian Perfection* and, not long after, his *Serious Call to a Devout and Holy Life*. Through that, seed was sown, which soon grew up and spread to Oxford, London, Bristol, Leeds, York, and, within a few years, to the greatest part of England, Scotland, and Ireland.

But how did the wisdom of God effect that great revival? The laborers He put into His harvest were beyond man's imagination. God chose the weak things to confound the strong, and the foolish things to confound the wise. He chose a few young, poor, ignorant men, with no experience, learning, or art, who were simple of heart, devoted to God, full of faith and zeal, seeking no honor, no profit, no pleasure, no ease, seeking merely to save souls. Fearing neither want, pain, persecution, nor whatever man could do unto them, not counting their lives dear unto themselves, they sought only to finish their charted course with joy. Of the same spirit were the lost people whom God, by their work, called out of darkness into His marvelous light. Many of them soon agreed to join together in order to strengthen one another's commitment to God. They were also simple of heart, devoted to God, zealous of good works, desiring neither honor, nor riches, nor pleasure, nor ease, nor anything under the sun but to attain the whole image of God, and to be with Him in glory.

But as these young preachers grew in years, they failed to grow in grace. Several of them increased in other knowledge, but not proportionately in the knowledge of God. They grew less simple, less alive to God, and less devoted to Him. They were less zealous for God, and, consequently, less active, less diligent in His service. Some of them began to desire the praise of men rather than only the praise of God. Some wearied of a traveling life, and sought ease and quietness. Some began again to fear the faces of men, and became ashamed of their calling, unwilling to deny themselves and to take up their cross daily to endure hardship as good soldiers of Jesus Christ.

Wherever these preachers labored, there was not much spiritual fruit. Their word was not, as it once was, clothed with power. It carried no demonstration of the Spirit with it. The same faintness of spirit was in their private conversation. They were no longer, in season or out of season, quick to warn and exhort everyone, so by any means they might save some. As some preachers declined from their first love of God, so did many of the people. They were likewise assaulted on every side, and encompassed with worldly temptations. While many of them triumphed over all, and were more than conquerors through Him who loved them, others gave way to the world, the flesh, or the devil, and fell into temptation. Some of them made shipwreck of their faith at once, others by slow, insensible degrees. Many, being in need of the necessities of life, were overwhelmed with the cares of the world. Many relapsed into the desire of things other than God, which choked the good seed, and it became unfruitful.

Of all temptations, none so struck at the whole work of God as the deceitfulness of riches, a thousand melancholy proofs of which I have seen during my fifty-year ministry. How deceitful indeed are riches! Who will ask you to believe they do God any good? Only a few—perhaps sixty, maybe not even half that—of the rich people I've known during my fifty years of ministry, as far as I can judge, were as holy being rich as they would have been had they been poor. By riches I do not mean great wealth, only more money than will obtain the conveniences of life. I account one a rich man who has food and clothing for himself and family without running into debt, with something left over. And how few are there in those circumstances who are not hurt, if not destroyed, by riches. Yet, who takes warning? Who seriously regards that awful declaration of Paul? Even they who desire to get rich fall into temptation and a snare, and into many foolish and hurtful desires that plunge men into destruction. How many sad instances have we seen of this throughout our ministry in all the large trading towns throughout the country where God has caused His spiritual power to be known. I have seen many of those who were once simple of heart, desiring nothing but God, now gratifying the desire of the flesh, studying to please their senses, particularly their tastes, endeavoring to increase the pleasure of eating insofar as possible.

Are you of that type? If indeed you are no drunkard or glutton, do you not indulge yourself in a kind of regular sensuality? Are not eating and drinking the greatest pleasures of your life, the most considerable part of your happiness? If so, I fear the Apostle Paul would have listed you among those whose god is their belly.

How many Christians are now again indulging the desire of the eye, using every means in their power to enlarge the pleasures of their imagination? If not in grandeur, which is beyond their means, yet in new or beautiful things. Are you not seeking happiness in buying pretty or elegant clothes, or furniture, or new experiences, or books, or art, or gardens?

"Why, what harm is there in these things?" you say. There is harm if they gratify the desire of the eye, and thereby strengthen and increase material thinking, making one more and more dead to God, and more alive to the world.

How many are indulging the pride of life, seeking the honor that comes from men by laying up treasures on earth? Many gain all they can, honestly and conscientiously. They save all they can by cutting off needless expense and adding frugality to diligence. All this is right—so far. This is the duty of everyone who fears God. However, they do not give all they can. Without that, they naturally grow more and more earthly-minded. Their affections will cleave to the wealth more and more, and they will have less and less communion with God.

Is this your situation? Do you seek the praise of men more than the praise of God? Do you lay up, or at least desire and endeavor to lay up, treasures on earth? Are you then, answer honestly, more and more alive to the world, and, consequently, more and more dead to God? It cannot be otherwise. Unless you give all you can, as well as gain and save all you can, there is no way to prevent your money from causing you to sink lower than the grave. The truth is, if any man loves the world, the love of the Father is not in him. To the man who loves God, if he slides into the love of the world, by the same degree the love of God will go out of his heart.

Perhaps there is something even more contained in the words, "Love not the world, neither the things that are in the world" (1 John 2:15). Here we are expressly warned against loving the world and the things of the world. The world is those who do not know God, who neither love nor fear Him. To love any of those with a love of delight or complacence, or to set our affections upon them is absolutely forbidden by our Lord. To have any fellowship with them further than necessary business requires, or in seeking to win them to the Lord, is equally forbidden. James labels friendship or intimacy with them as adultery. "Ye adulterers and adulteresses, know ye not, that the friendship of the world is enmity with God? Whosoever, therefore, will be a friend of the world, is the enemy of God" (James 4:4). Do not attempt to shuffle away or evade the meaning of those strong words. They plainly require us to stand aloof from the worldly, and to have no needless dealings with unholy people. Otherwise we shall surely backslide into conformity to the world, to its maxims, spirit, and customs. For not only their words, harmless as they seem, eat like a canker, but their very breath is infectious, their spirit imperceptibly influences our spirit. It steals like water into our hearts and like oil into our bones.

Christians with wealth are under a continual temptation to know and fellowship with worldly people. They are likewise under a continual temptation to pride, to think more highly of themselves than they ought. They are strongly tempted to revenge at the slightest provocation, and, having the means in their own hands, few resist the temptation. They are continually tempted to sloth, indolence, love of ease, softness, delicacy; to hatred of self-denial, and taking up the cross, even that of fasting and rising early.

If you have increased in wealth, do you find this true? Do you avoid fellowship with worldly men or do you spend more time with them than duty requires? Are you in no danger of pride or thinking yourself better than the poor and dirty? Do you ever resent or revenge an insult? Do you ever render evil for evil? Do you give way to laziness or love of ease? Do you deny yourself and take up your cross daily? Do you constantly rise as early as you did once? Why not? Is your soul not as precious now as it was then? How often do you fast? Is this not a duty to you, as much as to a day laborer? But if you are lacking in this, or any other respect, who will warn you? Who dares to tell you the plain truth, other than those who neither hope nor fear anything from you? If any try to deal directly with you, do you find it difficult to bear? Are you less reprovable, less advisable, than when you were poor?

Again, I challenge, having gained and saved all you can, do you give all you can? If you don't, your money will eat your flesh as fire and will sink you to the lowest hell! Oh, beware of laying up treasures upon earth! Is it not storing up wrath for the day of wrath?

Lord, I have warned them, but if they will not be warned, what more can I do? I can only give them up to their own hearts' lusts and let them follow their own imaginations.

By not taking this warning, it is certain many of the "Methodists" have already fallen. Many are falling at this very time, and there is great reason to believe that many more will fall—most of whom will rise no more.

But what method will the all-wise God take to repair the decay of His work? If He does not remove the light from this people, and raise up another people who will be more faithful to His grace, it is probable He will proceed in the same manner as He has done in the past. In the past, when any of the old preachers left their first love, lost their simplicity and zeal, and departed from their work, He raised up young men who are what their elders were, and sent them into the harvest in their place. He did the same when He was pleased to take any of His faithful laborers home. It is highly probable He will use the very same method in the future. In place of preachers who either die in the Lord or lose the spiritual life that God had given them, He will supply others who are alive to Him and desire only to live and die for Him.

Hear this, all you Christians, who have not the same life, the same communion with God, the same zeal for His cause, the same burning love for souls that you once had. Watch out that you do not lose the things you have worked for that you may be rewarded fully. Beware lest God swear in His wrath that you shall bear His standard no more, lest He be provoked to take the word of His grace utterly out of your mouth. Be assured the Lord has no need of you. His work does not depend upon anyone. As He is able, out of stones, to raise up children to Abraham, so He is able, out of the same, to raise up Christians after His own heart! Make haste and remember the height from which you are fallen. Repent and do the things you did at first!

Might not the Lord of the harvest lay you aside altogether if you despise the new laborers He has raised up merely because of their youth? This was regularly done to us when we were first sent out. Old, wise men asked, "What will these young heads do?" Are we going to have that same attitude? God forbid! Shall we tell God whom He shall send, and whom He shall employ in His own work? Are we then the ones in whom wisdom shall die? Does the work of God hang upon us? Oh, humble yourselves before God lest He pluck you away.

Let us review the method God in His wisdom used to continue the "Methodist" revival. After thousands of people who once ran well became overwhelmed with worldly care and riches, so that the faith they had received became weak, God constantly raised up men endued with the Spirit that the people had lost. Generally this change was an improvement, for these men were not only more numerous, but also more watchful, profiting by earlier examples. They were also more spiritual, more heavenly minded, more zealous, more alive to God, and more dead to earthly things.

And, blessed be God, we see He is now doing the same thing in various parts of the kingdom. In place of those who have fallen from their steadfastness, or are falling at this day, He is continually raising up others to be His children. This He does at one place or another, according to His own will, pouring out His living Spirit on other people just as it pleases Him. He is raising up those of every age and degree, young men and women, old men and children, to be a chosen generation, a royal priesthood, a holy nation, a peculiar people, to show forth His praise. He has called them out of darkness into His marvelous light. We have no reason to doubt He will continue to do so until His great promise is fulfilled—

that the earth will be filled with the knowledge of the glory of the Lord as the waters cover the sea, and all Israel will be saved after the full number of the Gentiles has come in.

But have all those who have sunk under manifold temptations fallen so low they can rise no more? Has the Lord cast them all off forever, receiving no more petitions? Has His promise come utterly to an end forevermore? God forbid that we should say this! Surely He is able to heal all their backslidings, for with God nothing is impossible.

Is He not willing to? He is God, and not man; therefore His mercy does not fail. Let no backslider despair. Return to the Lord and He will have mercy upon you; unto our God, and He will abundantly pardon (Isa. 55:7).

Meantime, the Lord says to you new Christian leaders, "Be not arrogant, but fear!" If the Lord spared not your older brother, be careful lest He not spare you! Fear God lest you fall by any of the same temptations, either the cares of the world, the deceitfulness of riches, or the desire for other things. You will be tempted in ten thousand different ways, perhaps as long as you remain in the body. But as long as you continue to watch and pray, you will not enter into temptations. His grace has always been sufficient for you, and so it will be to the end.

This is a short and general sketch of the manner wherein God works upon earth in repairing this work of grace wherever it is decayed through the subtlety of Satan and the unfaithfulness of men. Thus God is now carrying on His own work, and He will do so to the end of time. How wonderfully plain and simple is His general way of working—in the spiritual as well as the natural world. Yet as to our personal and numberless particulars, we must still cry out, "Oh, the depth! How unfathomable are His counsels, and His paths past tracing out!"

4

The Law and Its Use

Wherefore the law is holy, and the commandment holy, and just, and good. (Romans 7:12)

Perhaps there are few subjects within the whole area of Christianity so little understood as this scripture. The reader of Romans is usually told that by the law, Paul means only the Jewish law. Having no concern with that, he passes on with no further thought about it. Some are not satisfied with that interpretation. Seeing that the letter is written to the Romans, these people believe that Paul, in the beginning of this chapter, alludes to the old Roman law.

A careful observer of Paul's letter will not be content with either of these slight interpretations. The more one weighs the words, the more convinced he will be that Paul, by the law mentioned in this chapter, means neither the ancient law of Rome nor the ceremonial law of Moses. This clearly appears to all who carefully consider the tone of his letter. Paul begins the chapter, "Know ye not, brethren (for I speak to them that know the law), how that the law hath dominion over a man as long as he liveth?" (Rom. 7:1). Is this the law of Rome only, or the ceremonial law? No, surely it is the

---

Taken from John Wesley's, *Sermons on Several Occasions*, "The Original, Nature, Properties, and Use of the Law," XXXIV, Vol. 1, p. 306 ff.

moral law. To give an example, the woman who has a husband is bound by the moral law to her husband as long as he lives, but if the husband dies, she is loosed from her husband by the law. So if, while her husband lives, she marries another man, she shall be called an adulteress. If her husband is dead, she is free from that law, so that she is no adulteress even if she is married to another man.

From this particular example, Paul draws the reasonable conclusion, "Wherefore, my brethren, ye also are become dead to the law"—the whole Mosaic institution—"by the body of Christ," offered for you and bringing you under a new dispensation. Why? "That ye should [without any blame] be married to another, even to him who is raised from the dead," and has thereby given proof of his authority to make the change, "that we should bring forth fruit unto God" (Rom. 7:4). This we can do now, whereas before spiritual rebirth we could not.

When we were in the flesh, we were under the power of sin and our corrupt nature, which was necessarily the case until we knew the power of Christ's resurrection. The motions of human sins, which were by the law, broke out in various ways to bring forth evil fruit leading to death. But now we are delivered from the law, from the whole moral, as well as ceremonial, law. That entire legal institution is now, as it were, dead, and has no more authority over us than the husband when dead has over his wife. We should serve Him, who died for us and rose again, in newness of spirit, a new spiritual dispensation, and not in the oldness of the letter with a bare outward service, according to the letter of the Mosaic law.

Paul, having gone this far in proving that the Christian had set aside the Jewish law, and that the moral law itself, though it could never pass away, now stood on a different foundation than it did before, stops here to propose and answer an objection.

"What shall we say then? Is the law sin?" (Rom. 7:7). Some might infer this from a misunderstanding of the words "sinful passions aroused by the law." God forbid that we should say this, Paul said. The law is an irreconcilable enemy to sin, searching it out wherever it is. "I had not known sin but by the law: for I had not known lust, except the law had said, Thou shalt not covet" (Rom. 7:7). In the next verses, he adds this general conclusion, especially in regard to the moral law, from which the preceding instance was taken, "Wherefore the law is holy, and the commandment holy, and just, and good" (Rom. 7:12).

In order to explain and enforce these profound words, so little regarded because so little understood, I shall try to show the origin of this law, the nature of it, the essentials of it, that it is holy and just and good, and the uses of it.

The Origin of the Law

Moral law, often called "The law" to show its importance, is not, as some may possibly have supposed, from the time of Moses. Noah declared it to men long before Moses, and Enoch before him. But we may trace its origin higher still, even beyond the foundation of the world, to that period, unknown to men but doubtless enrolled in the annals of eternity, when the morning stars first sang together, being newly called into existence. It pleased the great Creator to make his first-born sons—the angels—intelligent beings, so that they might know Him who created them. For this purpose God gave them understanding to discern truth from falsehood and good from evil, and, as a necessary result of this, liberty, or a capacity for choosing the one and refusing the other. By this they were also enabled to offer Him a free and willing service, a service rewardable in itself, as well as most acceptable to their loving Master.

To use all the faculties that He had given, particularly understanding and liberty, He gave them a law, a complete model of all truth, intelligible and good, so far as angelic minds were capable of accepting. It was also the plan of their beneficent Creator by this to make possible a continual increase of their happiness, because every instance of obedience to His law would both add to the perfection of their nature and entitle them to a higher reward, which our righteous Judge would give in His time.

Later, God, in His appointed time, created a new order of intelligent beings by raising man from the dust of the earth. Breathing into him the breath of life, He caused him to become a living soul, endued with power to choose good or evil. He gave to this free, intelligent creature the same law He gave His angels. This law was not written on stone, or any corruptible substance, but engraved upon his heart by the touch of God. It was written in the inmost spirit both of men and of angels, so it might never be distant or hard to understand, but always at hand, always shining with clear light, as does the sun in heaven.

Such was the original law of God. With regard to man, the law was concurrent with his nature, but with regard to the angels, we see it came into being before the earth was made.

It was not long after man's creation that he rebelled against God, and, by breaking this moral law, almost erased it out of his heart. The eyes of his understanding were darkened in the same measure as his soul was, alienating him from the life of God. And yet God did not forsake the work of His own hands. Being reconciled to man through His Son in His love, God, in a measure, reinscribed the law on the heart of the dark and sinful man.

"He hath shewed thee, O man, what is good . . . even to do justly, and to love mercy, and to walk humbly with thy God" (Mic. 6:8).

This He showed, not only to Adam and Eve, but also to all their posterity, by that true light which enlightens every man who comes into the world. In spite of that light, all flesh had, in the process of time, corrupted their way before God, until He chose out of mankind a peculiar people, to whom He gave a more perfect knowledge of His law. Because they were slow to understand, He wrote the text of the law on two tables of stone. He then commanded the fathers to teach this to their children through all succeeding generations.

So it is that the law of God is now made known to those who do not know God. They hear, with the hearing of the ear, the instruction that was written before our time. But this is not enough. They cannot, by hearing, understand the height, and depth, and length, and breadth of it. Full revelation can be given only by God's Spirit. And so He gives this to all who truly believe, fulfilling that gracious promise made to all the Israel of God: "Behold, the days come, saith the Lord, that I will make a new covenant with the house of Israel. . . . This shall be the covenant that I will make . . . I will put my law in their inward parts, and write it in their hearts; and will be their God, and they shall be my people" (Jer. 31:31, 33).

The Nature of the Law

The nature of the law originally given to angels in heaven and man in paradise, and which God has so mercifully promised to write afresh in the hearts of all true believers, was the second thing I proposed to show. First I would comment that although the "law" and the "commandment" are sometimes differently taken, the commandment meaning but a part of the law, yet, in the text, they are used as equivalent terms, implying one and the same thing. We cannot understand here, either by one or the other, the ceremonial law. It is not the ceremonial law that Paul refers to in these words, "I had not known sin but by the law" (Rom. 7:7). This is too plain to need a proof. Neither is it the ceremonial law that says in the words immediately following, "Thou shalt not covet." Therefore the ceremonial law has no place in the present question.

Neither is the law mentioned in the text referring to the Mosaic dispensation. It cannot be so inferred in the text, for Paul never speaks highly about that imperfect and shadowy dispensation. He nowhere defines the Mosaic law as a spiritual law, or that it is holy and just and good. Neither is it true that God will write that law in the hearts of them whose iniquities He remembers no more. It is the moral law that is to be put into human hearts by Christ.

This law is an incorruptible picture of the high and holy One who inhabits eternity. It is He whom, in essence, no man has seen or can see, but is now made visible in this way to men and angels. Here is the face of God unveiled. Here is God manifested to His creatures as they are able to bear it, manifested to give and not to destroy life, that they may meet God and live. It is the heart of God disclosed to man. Yes, in some sense, what Paul says of Christ we may say about the law: It is the streaming forth, or out-beaming, of His glory, the express image of His person.

"If virtue," said the ancient heathen, "could assume such a shape that we could behold her with our eyes, what wonderful love would she excite in us!" The truth is, it is done already! The law of God is all virtues in one, in such a shape as to be beheld with open face by all those whose eyes God has enlightened. What is the law but divine virtue and wisdom assuming a visible form? What is it but the original ideas of truth and good, which were lodged in the uncreated mind from eternity, now drawn forth and clothed with such a vehicle as to appear even to human understanding?

If we consider the law of God from another point of view, it is supreme, unchangeable reason. It is unalterable moral virtue. It is the everlasting fitness of all things that are or ever were created. I am aware what a shortness, and even impropriety, there is in these and all other human expressions, when we endeavor by these faint pictures to shadow out the deep things of God. Nevertheless, we have no better, indeed no other way, during our infant state of existence. As we now know but in part, so we are required to prophesy (i.e., speak of the things of God) in part also. We cannot order our speech by reason of darkness, while we are in this house of clay. While I am a child, I must speak as a child, but I shall soon put away childish things, for when that which is perfect is come, that which is in part shall be done away.

The law of God, speaking after the manner of men, is a copy of the eternal mind, a transcript of His divine nature. It is the fairest offspring of the everlasting Father, the brightest flow of His essential wisdom, the visible beauty of the Most High. It is the delight and wonder of cherubim and seraphim, and all the company of heaven, and the glory and joy of every wise believer, every well-instructed child of God upon earth. Such is the nature of the ever blessed law of God.

Three Aspects of the Law

Next, I am to show certain essentials of the law. Here are three: It is holy, just, and good.

First of all, the law is holy. In the scripture mentioned at the top, Paul does not appear to speak of the law's effects, but rather of its nature. As James, speaking of the same thing under another name, says, "The wisdom that is from above," which is no other than this law, written in our heart, "is first pure, peaceable, gentle, and easy to be entreated, full of mercy and good fruits, without partiality, and without hypocrisy" (James 3:17). Consequently when it is transcribed into the life, as well as the soul, it is, as the same apostle terms it, pure religion and undefiled, or the pure, clean, unpolluted worship of God.

It is, indeed, in the highest degree, pure, chaste, clean, holy. Otherwise it could not be the immediate offspring, and much less the express resemblance of God, who is essential holiness. It is pure from all sin, clean and unspotted from any touch of evil. It is a chaste virgin, incapable of any defilement, of any mixture with that which is unclean or unholy. It has no fellowship with sin of any kind, for what communion has light with darkness? As sin is, in its very nature enmity to God, so His law is enmity to sin.

Therefore the apostle rejects with abhorrence the blasphemous speculation that the law of God is either sin itself, or the cause of sin. God forbid that we should imagine it is the cause of sin; rather, it is the discoverer of it, because it detects the hidden things of darkness and drags them out into open day. By this means, sin appears in truth to be sin. All its disguises are torn away, and it appears in its native deformity. Sin by the commandment becomes exceedingly sinful. Being now committed in light and knowledge, stripped even of the poor plea of ignorance, it loses all excuse, as well as disguise, and becomes even more odious to God and man.

It is also true that sin works death by that which is good, which in itself is pure and holy. When it is dragged into light, sin rages much more. When sin is restrained, it bursts out with greater violence. Paul, as a person who was convinced of sin but not yet delivered from it, speaks of sin seizing the opportunity by the commandment. Paul tried to restrain it; but sin, disdaining the restraint, produced in him every kind of covetous desire which that commandment sought to restrain. When the commandment came, sin revived. It fretted and raged. But this is no condemnation of the commandment. Though it is abused, it cannot be defiled. This only proves that the heart of man is desperately wicked, and the law of God is holy still.

Second, His law is just. It renders to all their due. It prescribes exactly what is right, precisely what ought to be done, said or thought—regarding the Creator of our being, ourselves, and every creature He has made. It is adapted, in all respects, to the nature of things, of the whole universe, and every individual. It is suited to all the circumstances of each, and to all their mutual relations, whether such as have existed from the beginning, or commenced in any following period. It is exactly agreeable to the fitness of things, whether essential or accidental. It clashes with none of these in any degree, nor is ever unconnected with them. If the Scripture be taken in that sense, there is nothing arbitrary in the law of God. The whole and every part thereof is totally dependent upon His will, so that "Thy will be done" is the supreme universal law, both in earth and heaven.

But is the will of God the cause of His law? Is His will the origin of right and wrong? Is a thing therefore right because God wills it? Or does He will it because it is right?

This celebrated question is more curious than useful. In the manner it is usually asked, it has not the respect due from a creature to the Creator and Governor of all things. It is hardly decent for man to require the supreme God to give an account of himself. Nevertheless, in awe and reverence, we may speak a little. God forgive us if we speak amiss!

It seems as if the whole difficulty arises from considering God's will as distinct from God. None can doubt that God is the cause of the law of God, and the will of God is God himself. Consequently, to say the will of God, or God himself, is the cause of the law is one and the same thing.

Again, if the law, the immutable rule of right and wrong, depends on the nature and fitness of things, and on their essential relation to each other, then it must depend on God, or the will of God, because those things themselves, with all their relations, are the works of His hands. By His will, for His pleasure alone, they all are and were created (Rev. 4:11).

Yet it may be granted, which is probably all that a considerate person would contend for, that in every particular case, God wills this or that (i.e., that men should honor their parents) because it is right, agreeable to the fitness of things, and to the relation wherein they stand.

Third, the law is also good. This we may easily infer from the fountain from which it flowed, the goodness of God. What but goodness alone inclined Him to impart that divine copy of himself to the holy angels? To what, other than His goodness, can we impute His bestowing upon us the character of His own nature? What but tender love caused Him afresh to manifest His will to fallen man, either to Adam or any of his offspring, who like Adam were far short of the glory of God? Was it not mere love that moved Him to publish His law after man's understanding went so far astray? And that very love caused Him to send His prophets to declare that law to the blind, thoughtless children of men.

Doubtless, it was His goodness that raised up Enoch and Noah to be preachers of righteousness; and that same goodness caused Abraham, His friend, and Isaac and Jacob to bear witness to the truth. It was His goodness alone, which, when the thick darkness of the people had covered the earth, gave a written law to Moses, and through him gave it to the nation God chose. It was love that explained these living oracles by David and all the prophets that followed. Then when the fullness of time had come, God sent His only begotten Son, not to destroy the law, but to fulfill and confirm every jot and tittle of it, till, having written it in the hearts of all His children, and put all His enemies under His feet, He shall deliver up the kingdom to the Father that God may be all in all.

And this law, which the goodness of God gave at first and has preserved through all ages, is like the fountain from which it springs—full of goodness and benevolence. It is mild and kind. It is, as expressed in the Psalms, sweeter than honey and the honeycomb (Ps. 19:10). It is winning and amiable. It includes whatsoever things are lovely or of good report. If there be any virtue, if there be any praise before God and His holy angels, they are all comprised in this, wherein are hid all the treasures of the divine wisdom, and knowledge, and love.

The law is good in its effects, as well as in its nature. As the tree is, so are its fruits. The fruits of the law of God written in the heart are righteousness, and peace, and assurance forever. Or rather, the law itself is righteousness, filling the soul with a peace that passes all understanding, causing us to rejoice evermore in the testimony of a good conscience toward God. The law is not so properly a pledge, as an advance on our inheritance, being a part of the purchased possession. It is God made manifest in our flesh and bringing with Him eternal life, assuring us by that pure and perfect love that we are sealed unto the day of redemption. He will spare us as a man spares his own son who serves him, and in that day when He makes up His jewels, there remains for us a crown of glory that does not fade away.

It remains only to show, in the fourth and last place, the uses of the law. The first, without question, is to *convince the world of sin*. This is the peculiar work of the Holy Spirit, who can work it without any means at all, or by whatever means it pleases Him. Accordingly, there are some whose hearts have been broken in pieces in a moment, either in sickness or in health, without any visible cause or any outward means whatsoever. Others have been awakened to a sense of the wrath of God abiding on them by hearing that God was in Christ, reconciling the world unto himself. But it is the general practice of the Spirit of God to convict sinners by the law. It is this which, being pressed on the conscience, generally breaks the rocks in pieces. It is more especially this part of the Word of God that is quick and powerful, full of life and energy, and sharper than any two-edged sword. This, in the hand of God and of those whom He has sent, pierces through all the folds of a deceitful heart and divides even the soul and the spirit, and, as it were, the very joints and marrow. By this is the sinner discovered to himself. All his fig leaves are torn away, and he sees that he is wretched, and poor, and miserable, and blind, and naked. The law flashes conviction on every side. He feels himself a mere sinner. He has nothing to say. His mouth is stopped, and he stands guilty before God.

To slay the sinner is then the first use of the law; to destroy the life and strength in which he trusts, and to convince him that he is dead while he lives, not only under the sentence of death, but actually dead unto God, void of all spiritual life, dead in trespasses and sins.

The second use of it is to *bring him into life*, into Christ, that he may live. It is true, in performing both of these offices, that the law acts as a severe schoolmaster. It drives us by force, rather than draws us by love; yet love is the spring of all. It is the spirit of love, which, by this painful means, tears away our confidence in ourselves, which leaves us no broken reed in which to trust, and causes the sinner, stripped of all, to cry out in the bitterness of his soul, or groan in the depth of his heart, "I give up every plea except, Lord, I am damned; but Thou hast died."

The third use of the law is to *keep us alive*. It is the grand means whereby the blessed Spirit prepares the believer for larger communications of the life of God.

I am afraid this great and important truth is little understood not only by the world but even by many real children of God by faith. Many of these wrongly declare that when we come to Christ, we are done with the law, and that, in this sense, Christ is the end of the law to everyone who believes. So He is righteousness and justification to everyone who believes. In Christ, they say, the law comes to an end. It justifies none, but only brings the sinner to Christ. So Jesus is, in another respect, the end or scope of the law, the point at which it continually aims. But in truth however, the law goes further than this, namely, to keep us with Him. For it is continually encouraging all believers, the more they see of its height, and depth, and length, and breadth, to exhort one another so much the more.

> Closer and closer let us cleave
> To His beloved embrace;
> Expect His fullness to receive,
> And grace to answer grace.

Let us look at this a little closer. It is correct that every believer can disregard the law as far as the Jewish ceremonial law is concerned, as well as the entire Mosaic dispensation, for Christ has taken these out of the way. We also agree we are finished with the moral law as a means of procuring our justification, for we are justified freely by His grace through the redemption that is in Jesus. However, in another sense we are not done with this law, for it is still of extensive use.

First, the law convinces of any sin that may yet remain in our hearts and lives, and thereby keeps us closer to Christ, so His blood may cleanse us every moment. Second, we derive strength from our Head into ourselves, whereby He empowers us to do what His law commands. Third, we are confirmed in our hope of receiving grace upon grace till we are in actual possession of the fullness of His promises for obedience to the law.

How clearly does this agree with the experience of believers. While we have cried out, "Oh, what love I have unto your law. All the day long is my study in it," we have seen through this divine mirror, more and more of our own personal sinfulness—that neither our heart nor our ways are right before God—and that realization sent us to Christ, our spiritual liberator. This shows the meaning of what is written, "Thou shalt make a plate of pure gold, and grave upon it, like the engravings of a signet, HOLINESS TO THE LORD. And it shall be upon Aaron's forehead, that Aaron may bear the iniquity of the holy things, which the children of Israel shall hallow in all their holy gifts; and it shall be always upon his forehead, that they may be accepted before the Lord" (Ex. 28:36, 38).

To explain this by a single example, the law says you shall not kill, and hereby, as our Lord teaches, forbids not only outward acts but every unkind word or thought. Now the more I look into this perfect law, the more I feel how far I come short of it. The more I feel this, the more I feel my need of His blood to atone for all my sin, and of His Spirit to purify my heart and make me perfect and entire, lacking nothing.

Therefore, I cannot spare the law one moment, no more than I can spare Christ, seeing I now want it as much to keep me close to Christ as I ever wanted it to bring me to Him. Otherwise, my evil heart of unbelief would immediately depart from the living God. Indeed, each is continually sending me to the other—the law to Christ, and Christ to the law. On the one hand, the height and depth of the law constrain me to fly to the love of God in Christ, on the other, the love of God in Christ endears the law to me, above gold or precious stones, seeing I know every part of it is a gracious promise that my Lord will fulfill in its season.

Who are you, then, to judge the law and speak evil of the law, ranking it with sin, Satan, and death, and send all to hell? The Apostle James rated speaking evil of the law so enormous a piece of wickedness that he knew not how to aggravate the guilt of judging our brothers more than by showing it included this. He says, "Thou art not a doer of the law, but a judge" (James 4:11), a judge of that which God has ordained to judge you. So you have set up yourself in the judgment seat of Christ, and cast down the rule whereby He will judge the world. Observe what advantage Satan has gained over you, and never again think or speak lightly of, much less dress up as a scarecrow, this blessed instrument of the grace of God. Yes, love and value it for the sake of Him from whom it came, and of Him to whom it leads. Let it be your glory and joy, next to the cross of Christ. Declare its praise and make it honorable before all men.

If you are thoroughly convinced that the law is the off-spring of God, that it is the copy of all His inimitable per-fections, and that it is holy, and just, and good, especially to them who believe, then instead of casting it away as a pol-luted thing, see that you grasp it more firmly. Never let the law of mercy and truth, of love to God and man, of lowliness, meekness, and purity forsake you. Bind it about your neck, write it on the table of your heart. Keep close to the law, if you will keep close to Christ. Hold it fast, do not let it go. Let this continually lead you to Jesus' atoning blood, contin-ually confirm your hope, till all the righteousness of the law is fulfilled in you and you are filled with the fullness of God.

If the Lord has already fulfilled His Word, if He has al-ready written His law in your heart, then stand fast in the liberty wherewith Christ has made you free. You are not only made free from Jewish ceremonies, from the guilt of sin, and the fear of hell, but from what is infinitely more—the power of sin, serving the devil, and offending God. Stand fast in this liberty, in comparison of which all the rest is not even worthy to be named. Stand fast in loving God with all your heart, and serving Him with all your strength. This is perfect freedom, thus to keep His law and to walk in all His command-ments blameless.

Be not entangled again with the yoke of bondage. I do not mean of Jewish bondage, nor yet of bondage to the fear of hell. These, I trust, are far from you. But beware of being entangled again with the yoke of sin, of any inward or out-ward transgression of the law. Abhor sin far more than death or hell. Abhor sin itself far more than the punishment of it. Beware of the bondage of pride, of desire, of anger, of every evil temper, or word, or work. Look unto Jesus, and to do this, look more and more into the perfect law, the law of liberty, and continue in it. Then shall you grow daily in grace, and in the knowledge of our Lord Jesus Christ.

5

The Law Established Through Faith

Do we then make void the law through faith? God forbid: yea, we establish the law. (Romans 3:31)

There are several ways the Church has made the law void through faith. The first is by not preaching it at all. This effectually makes it all void at a stroke. Doing this under pretense of preaching Christ and magnifying the gospel is, in truth, destroying both the law and the gospel.

The second way is by teaching, whether directly or indirectly, that faith replaces the necessity of holiness, and that holiness is less necessary now, or less necessary, than before Christ came, or that it is less necessary to us than it otherwise would have been because we believe in Him; or that Christian liberty is a liberty from any kind or degree of holiness now that we are under the covenant of grace and not of works. Such teaching, which voids the law, says, A man is justified by faith without the works of the law, and that "to him that worketh not, but believeth . . . his faith is counted for righteousness" (Rom. 4:5).

Taken from John Wesley's, *Sermons on Several Occasions*, "The Law Established Through Faith," XXXVI, Vol. 1, p. 323 ff.

Third, making void the law in practice, though not in principle, by living or acting as if faith were designed to excuse us from holiness, allowing ourselves to sin because we are not under the law, but under grace. It remains to ask how we may follow a better pattern, how we may be able to say with Paul, "Do we then make void the law through faith? God forbid: yea, we establish the law."

We do not, of course, establish the old ceremonial law. We know that it was abolished forever. Much less do we establish the whole Mosaic dispensation. This we know our Lord has nailed to His cross. Nor yet do we establish the moral law, as if the fulfilling of it, the keeping of all the commandments, were the condition of our justification. If that were so, surely no man living would be justified in God's sight. Admitting all this, we still, in Paul's sense, establish the law, the moral law.

Declare the Whole Truth!

We establish the law first by our doctrine, by endeavoring to preach it in its whole extent, to explain and enforce every part of it in the same manner as Jesus did while on earth. We establish it by following Peter's advice, "If any man speak, let him speak as the oracles of God," as the holy men of old, moved by the Holy Spirit, spoke and wrote for our instruction; and as the apostles of our blessed Lord by the direction of the same Spirit. We establish it whenever we speak in His name, by keeping back nothing from those who hear, by declaring to them, without any limitation or reserve, the whole counsel of God. To more effectively establish it, we use great plainness of speech. We are not like many who corrupt the Word of God, as deceitful men do their bad wines. We do not mix, adulterate, or soften the truth to make it suit the taste of the hearers, but in sincerity and of God, in the sight of God, we speak in Christ, as having no other aim than, by manifestation of the truth, to commend ourselves to every man's conscience in the sight of God.

Thus, by our doctrine, we establish the law when we openly declare it to all men in the fullness in which it was delivered by our blessed Lord and His apostles. We follow their example when we speak of the law in its height, and depth, and length, and breadth. We then establish the law when we declare every part of it, every commandment contained in it. We do this not only in its full, literal sense, but also in its spiritual meaning, and not only with regard to the outward actions, which it either forbids or requires, but also with respect to the inward principle—to the thoughts, desires, and intents of the heart.

And indeed we do this more diligently, because as important as these things are, they are little considered or understood. In fact, so little is understood that we may truly say of the law, when taken in its full spiritual meaning, it is a mystery which was hidden from ages and generations since the world began.

It was utterly hidden from the pagan world. They, with all their boasted wisdom, neither found God, nor the law of God, either in the letter or much less in the spirit of it. Their foolish hearts were more and more darkened. While professing themselves wise, they became fools.

It was almost equally hidden, as to its spiritual meaning, from the bulk of the Jewish nation. Even those who were so ready to declare concerning others, "This people who knoweth not the law are cursed" (John 7:49), pronounced their own sentence, being under the same curse with the same dreadful ignorance. Witness to this is our Lord's continual reproof of the wisest among them, for their gross misinterpretations of it. More witness is the supposition almost universally received among them, that they needed only to make clean the outside of the cup, that paying the tithe of mint, anise, and cummin—outward exactness—would atone for inward unholiness, their total neglect both of justice and mercy, and of faith and the love of God. So absolutely was the spiritual meaning of the law hidden from the wisest of them that one of their most eminent rabbis commented incorrectly on those words of the psalm, "If I regard iniquity in my heart, the Lord will not hear me" (Ps. 66:18). The rabbi said if it were only in the heart, if no outward wickedness were committed, the Lord would not pay any attention to it; He would not punish unless the outward act were committed.

But, alas, the law of God, as to its inward, spiritual meaning, is not only hidden from the Jews or heathens or those lands covered with the darkness and ignorance of Rome, but it is even hidden from what is called the Christian world, at least from a vast majority of it. The spiritual sense of the commandments of God is still a mystery to many in those places as well. It is certain that the far greater part, even of those who are called "reformed Christians," are utter strangers at this day to the law of Christ—its purity and spirituality.

So even in our times, "the scribes and the Pharisees," the men who have the form but not the power of religion, who are generally wise in their own eyes and righteous in their own conceits, upon hearing these things are deeply offended when we speak of the religion of the heart. They are particularly offended when we show that without this were we to give all our goods to feed the poor, it would profit us nothing. But offended they must be, for we cannot but speak the truth as it is in Jesus. It is our part, whether they will hear or whether they will refuse, to deliver our own soul. We are to declare all that is written in the book of God, not as pleasing men, but the Lord. We are to declare not only all the promises but all the threatenings that we find therein. At the same time that we proclaim all the blessings and privileges God has prepared for us, we teach every thing He has commanded. We know that all His commandments have their use, either for the awakening of those who sleep, the instructing of the ignorant, the comforting of the feebleminded, or the building up and perfecting of the saints. We know that all Scripture is given by the inspiration of God, and is profitable either for doctrine or for reproof, either for correction or for instruction in righteousness. The man of

God, in the process of the work of God in his soul, has need of every part thereof that he may at length be perfect, thoroughly furnished with all good works.

It is our responsibility to preach Christ by proclaiming all the things He has revealed. We may indeed, without blame, and with a peculiar blessing from God, declare the love of our Lord Jesus Christ. We may speak, in a more special manner, of the Lord our righteousness. We may speak about the grace of God in Christ, reconciling the world unto himself. We may, at proper opportunities, praise Him as bearing the iniquities of us all, as being wounded for our transgressions, and being bruised for our iniquities, so that by His stripes we might be healed. Still, we would not be preaching Christ according to His Word, if we confined ourselves to this alone. We are not ourselves clear before God unless we proclaim Him in *all* His offices. If we are truly workmen who need not be ashamed, we must preach Christ as more than our great High Priest, taken from among men and ordained for men to reconcile us to God by His blood, and ever living to make intercession for us.

We must also make clear that He is the prophet of the Lord, who of God is made unto us wisdom. By His Word and His Spirit, He is always with us, guiding us into all truth. As a king forever, He is giving laws to all whom He has bought with His blood, restoring those to the image of God whom He had first reinstated in His favor, reigning in all believing hearts until He has subdued all things to himself, until He has utterly cast out all sin and brought in everlasting righteousness.

Faith Leads Us to Love

We establish the law when we so preach faith in Christ as not to replace, but to produce, holiness, all manner of holiness, in the heart and life.

In order to do this, we continually declare that faith itself, even Christian faith—the faith of God's elect, the faith of the operation of God—still is only the handmaiden of love. As glorious and honorable as it is, faith is not the end of the commandment. God has given this honor to love alone. Love is the end of all the commandments of God. Love is the end, the sole end, of every dispensation of God, from the beginning of the world to the consummation of all things. It will endure when heaven and earth flee away, for love alone never fails.

Wonderful things are spoken about faith, and whoever partakes of it may well say with Paul, "Thanks be unto God for his unspeakable gift" (2 Cor. 9:15). Yet still it loses all its excellence when brought into a comparison with love. What Paul declares about the superior glory of the gospel, over that of the law, may also be spoken of the superiority of love over faith. Even that which was made glorious has no glory in this respect, by reason of the glory that excels. All the glory of faith arises hence, that it ministers to love. Faith is the temporary means that God has ordained to promote the eternal end, love.

Let those who magnify faith beyond all proportion, so as to swallow up all other things, and who so totally misunderstand the nature of it as to imagine it stands in the place of love, consider further. As love will exist after faith, so it existed long before it. The angels, who from the moment of their creation beheld the face of their Father who is in heaven, had no occasion for faith, in its general notion, as it is the evidence of things not seen. Neither had they need of faith, in its more particular acceptance, faith in the blood of Jesus. For He took not upon Him the nature of angels, but only the seed of Abraham. There was, therefore, no place before the foundation of the world for faith, either in the general or particular sense, but there was for love. Love existed from eternity, in God the great ocean of love. Love had a place in all the children of God, from the moment of their creation. They received at once from their gracious Creator life and love.

Nor is it certain, as ingeniously and plausibly as many have speculated, that faith, even in the general sense of the word, had any place in paradise. It is highly probable, from that short and uncircumstantial account that we have in Holy Scripture, that Adam, before he rebelled against God, walked with Him by sight and not by faith. He was then able to talk with Him face to face, whose face we cannot now see and live. As a consequence, he had no need of that faith whose purpose it is to supply the lack of sight.

On the other hand, it is absolutely certain that faith, in its particular sense, then had no place. For in that sense, it necessarily presupposes sin, and the wrath of God declared against the sinner, without which there is no need of an atonement for sin in order for the sinner's reconciliation with God. Consequently, as there was no need of an atonement before the Fall, so there was no place for faith in that atonement. Man then was pure from every stain of sin, holy as God is holy. Yet even then, love filled His heart. It reigned in Him without a rival. It was only when love was lost by sin that faith was added, not for its own sake, nor with any design that it should exist any longer than until it had answered the end for which it was ordained, namely, to restore man to the love from which he was fallen. At the Fall, therefore, was added this evidence of things unseen, which before was utterly needless, this confidence in redeeming love, which could not possibly have any place till the promise was made that the seed of the woman should bruise the serpent's head.

Faith, then, was originally designed by God to reestablish the law of love. Therefore, in speaking thus, we are not undervaluing it, or robbing it of its due praise, but, on the contrary, showing its real worth, exalting it in its just proportion and giving it that very place that the wisdom of God assigned it from the beginning. It is the grand means of restoring that holy love wherein man was originally created. It follows that although faith is of no value in itself, it leads to the establishing anew of the law of love in our hearts. In the present state of things, it is the only means under heaven for accomplishing that. It is on that account an absolute blessing to man, and of unlimited value before God.

Next, this naturally brings us to observe the most important way of establishing the law—establishing it in our own hearts and lives. Without this, what would all the rest avail? We might establish it by our doctrine, we might preach it in its whole extent, and we might explain and enforce every part of it. We might open it in its most spiritual meaning, and declare the mysteries of the kingdom. We might preach Christ in all His offices, and faith in Christ as opening all the treasures of His love. We can do all this, yet, if the law we preached were not established in our hearts, we should be of no more account before God than sounding brass or tinkling cymbals. All our preaching would be so far from profiting ourselves that it would only increase our damnation.

Therefore, the main point to be considered is how we may establish the law in our own hearts, so that it may have its full influence on our lives. This can be done only by faith.

Faith Leads to Holiness

It is faith alone that effectually produces this end. As long as we walk by faith, not by sight, we go swiftly on in the way of holiness. While we steadily look not at the things that are seen but at those that are not seen, we are more and more crucified to the world, and the world crucified to us. When the eye of the soul is constantly fixed, not on the things that are temporal, but on those that are eternal, our affections are more and more loosened from earth and fixed on things above. So faith, in general, is the most direct and effective means of promoting all righteousness and true holiness, of establishing the holy and spiritual law in the hearts of those who believe.

By faith, taken in its more particular meaning (confidence in a pardoning God), we establish His law in our own hearts in a still more effective manner. There is no other motive that so powerfully inclines us to love God as the sense of the love of God in Christ. Nothing except a piercing conviction of this could enable us to give our hearts to Him who was given for us. From this principle of grateful love to God arises love to our brother also.

We cannot avoid loving our neighbor if we truly believe the love with which God has loved us. Now this love to man, grounded on faith and love to God, works no ill to our neighbor. Consequently it is, as Paul observes, the fulfilling of the whole negative law. For this, you shall not commit adultery. You shall not kill. You shall not steal. You shall not bear false witness. You shall not covet. If there is any other commandment, it is briefly included in this saying, you shall love your neighbor as yourself.

Neither is love content with barely working no evil to our neighbor. It continually incites us to do good, as we have time and opportunity, in every possible way and in every possible degree to all men. It is, therefore, the fulfilling of the positive as well as of the negative law of God. Nor does faith fulfill the external part of the law only. It also works inwardly by love, purifying the heart and cleansing it from all vile affections. Everyone who has this faith purifies himself even as He is pure, purifies himself from every earthly, sensual desire, from all vile and inordinate affections, and from the whole of that carnal mind that is enmity against God. At the same time, if love does its perfect work, it fills him with all goodness, righteousness, and truth. It brings all heaven into his soul and causes him to walk in the light, even as God is in the light.

Grow in Grace, Grow in God

Let us try to establish the law in ourselves, using all the power we receive from grace to fulfull all righteousness. Calling to mind what light we received from God while His Spirit was convincing us of sin, let us beware we do not put out that light. What we had then attained, let us hold fast. Let nothing induce us to rebuild the old nature we have destroyed, or to resume anything, small or great, which we then clearly saw was not for the glory of God or the profit of our own soul. We should neglect nothing, small or great, which before we could not neglect without a check from our own conscience. To increase and perfect the light we had before, let us add the light of faith. Now we confirm the former gift of God by a deeper sense of whatever He had then shown us, with a greater tenderness of conscience and a more exquisite sensibility of sin. Walking now with joy, and not fear, in a clear, steady sight of things eternal, we look upon pleasure, wealth, praise—all the things of earth—like bubbles upon the water, counting nothing important, nothing desirable, nothing worth a deliberate thought, except what is within the veil, where Jesus sits at the right hand of God.

Can you say to Him, "You are merciful to my unrighteousness; my sins you remember no more"? Then, see that you fly from sin like you would from the face of a serpent. For how exceedingly sinful unrighteousness appears to you now. How heinous it is above all expression. On the other hand, in how agreeable a light do you now see the holy and perfect will of God. Now, therefore, labor that His will may be fulfilled in you, by you, and upon you.

Watch and pray that you may sin no more, that you may see and shun the least transgression of His law. Like the specks of dust you can see when the sun shines into a dark place, so now you can see the sins you could not see before because the Sun of Righteousness shines in your heart.

Do all diligence to walk, in every respect, according to the light you have received. Be zealous to receive more light daily, more of the knowledge and love of God, more of the Spirit of Christ, more of His life and of the power of His resurrection. Use all the knowledge, and love, and life, and power you have already attained, so you shall continually go on from faith to faith. You shall daily increase in holy love till faith is swallowed up in sight, and the law of love is established to all eternity.

6

The Righteousness of Faith

*Moses describeth the righteousness which is of the law,
That the man which doeth those things shall live by them.
But the righteousness which is of faith speaketh on this wise,
Say not in thine heart, Who shall ascend into heaven? (that
is, to bring Christ down from above:) Or, Who shall descend
into the deep? (that is, to bring up Christ again from the
dead.) But what saith it? The word is nigh thee, even in thy
mouth, and in thy heart: that is, the word of faith, which we
preach. (Romans 10:5–8)*

Here Paul is not comparing the covenant given by Moses
to the covenant given by Jesus. If we ever thought this, it
was because of failure to observe that part of these words
were spoken by Moses to the people of Israel concerning their
covenant that was then in effect. But Paul is here comparing
the covenant of grace through Christ, established for men in
all ages, to the covenant of works made with Adam. In Paul's
time, many supposed Adam's covenant to be the only one
that God had made with man. This was particularly so of the
Jews about whom Paul writes.

It was to those Jews that he so affectionately spoke in the

Taken from John Wesley's, *Sermons on Several Occasions*, "The Righteousness of Faith," VI, Vol. 1, p. 53ff.

beginning of this chapter. "My heart's desire and prayer to God for Israel is, that they might be saved. For I bear them record that they have a zeal of God, but not according to knowledge. For they being ignorant of God's righteousness [of the justification that flows from His grace and mercy, freely forgiving our sins through the Son of His love, through the redemption in Jesus], and going about to establish their own righteousness [their own holiness, prior to faith in Him who justifies the ungodly, as the ground of their pardon and acceptance], have not submitted themselves unto the righteousness of God" (Rom. 10:1–3). Consequently, they find death in the error of their life.

They were ignorant of the truth that Christ is the end of the law for righteousness to everyone who believes. By giving himself once, He put an end to the first law or covenant. Indeed, this was not given by God to Moses. It was given to Adam in his state of innocence. God's strict meaning was, do this and live. At the same time, Jesus purchased for us that better covenant: believe and live. Believe and you will be saved—saved now both from the guilt and the power of sin, and later from its wages.

Many, even those who are called Christians, are similarly ignorant now. Many have a zeal for God, yet lacking proper knowledge, still seek works to establish their own righteousness and earn their pardon and acceptance. Because of that error, they steadily refuse to submit themselves to Jesus, the righteousness of God.

My heart's desire and prayer to God for you is that you may be saved. To remove this great stumbling block from your path, I shall attempt to show both the righteousness of the law and the righteousness of faith. I shall also point out the folly of trusting in the law and the wisdom of submitting to the righteousness of faith.

The Requirements of the Law

First, the righteousness of the law says the man who does these things shall live by them. Constantly and perfectly observe and do all these things; then you shall live forever. This law, or covenant, usually called the covenant of works, was given by God to man in the beginning. It required perfect obedience in all parts, entire and lacking nothing. This was the condition of man's eternal continuance in the holiness and happiness in the original creation.

The law required that man should fulfill all righteousness, inward and outward, negative and positive. He should not only abstain from every idle word, and avoid every evil work, but should also keep every affection, every desire, and every thought in obedience to the will of God. He should continue this holiness, as He who had created him was holy in heart and in all manner of conversation. He should be pure in heart even as God is pure, perfect as his Father in heaven is perfect. He should love the Lord his God with all his heart, with all his soul, with all his mind, and with all his strength. He should love every soul that God had made, even as God had loved him. By this universal benevolence, he should dwell in God, who is love, and God in him. He should serve the Lord his God with all his strength, and in all things singly aim at His glory.

All these were the things that the righteousness of the law required, that those who did them might live. But it further required that this entire obedience to God, this inward and outward holiness, this conformity both of heart and life to His will, should be perfect in the highest degree. No abatement or allowance could possibly be made for falling short in any degree, any jot or tittle, either of the outward or the inward law. Even if every commandment relating to outward things was obeyed, that was not adequate unless every one was obeyed with the whole strength, in the highest measure and the most perfect manner. Neither did it answer the demand of this covenant to love God with every power and faculty unless He were loved with the full capacity of each, with the total commitment of the soul.

One additional thing was absolutely required by the righteousness of the law. That was his continual obedience.

Man's perfect holiness of heart and life should be perfectly uninterrupted. It should continue without any interruption from the moment when God created man and breathed into him the breath of life until the days of this life ended and he be given life everlasting.

The righteousness, then, which is of the law, speaks this way: You, oh man of God, stand fast in love, in the image of God in which you are made. If you will remain in life, keep the commandments that are now written in your heart. Love, as yourself, every soul that He has made. Desire nothing but God. Aim at God in every thought, in every word, in every work. Swerve not in one motion of body or soul from Him, your mark, and the prize of your high calling. Let all that is in you praise His holy name, every power and faculty of your soul, in every kind, in every degree, and at every moment of your existence. This do and you shall live. Your light shall shine, your love shall flame more and more, till you are received up into the house of God in the heavens to reign with Him forever and ever.

The Righteousness of Faith

But the righteousness that is of faith speaks another way: Do not ask who shall ascend into heaven, that is, to bring Christ down from above, as though it were some impossible task, which God required you previously to perform, in order to win acceptance. Do not ask who shall descend into the deep, that is, to bring Christ up from the dead, as though that were still remaining to be done. What it says is, the Word, according to the meaning by which you may now be accepted as an heir of life eternal, is near you, as near as your mouth and your heart. That is the word of faith, which we preach, the new covenant that God has now established with sinful man through Christ Jesus.

"The righteousness which is of faith" means that condition of justification, and, consequently, of present and final salvation if we endure to the end, which was given by God to fallen man through the merits and mediation of His only begotten Son. This was in part revealed to Adam soon after his fall, being contained in the original promise made to him and his posterity, concerning who should "bruise the serpent's head." This was a little more clearly revealed to Abraham by the angel of God from heaven, who said, "By myself have I sworn, saith the Lord, that in thy seed shall all the nations of the world be blessed" (Gen. 22:16).

It was more fully made known to Moses, to David, and to the prophets who followed, and through them to many of the people of God in their respective generations. Yet even the bulk of these were ignorant of it, and very few understood it clearly. So, life and immortality were not as brightly shown to the Jews of old as they are now to us, by the gospel.

Now this new covenant does not say to sinful man, "Perform unsinning obedience, and live." If this were the case, we would have no more benefit of all that Jesus has done and suffered for us than if we were required, in order to live, to ascend into heaven and bring down Christ from above, or to descend into the deep, into the invisible world, and bring up Christ from the dead. It does not require anything impossible to be done. That would only mock human weakness. To mere man, what it requires would be impossible, but to man assisted by the Spirit of God, it is not.

Indeed, strictly speaking, the covenant of grace does not require us to do anything at all, as absolutely and indispensably necessary, in order to obtain justification. It only requires we believe in Him, who for the sake of His Son and the atoning sacrifice that Jesus has made, justifies the ungodly, whose works are inadequate, and imputes His faith to him for righteousness. Even so, Abraham believed in the Lord and God counted it to him for righteousness. Then he received the sign of circumcision, a seal of righteousness of faith, that he might be the father of all who believe, so his righteousness might be attributed to them also.

What does the covenant say of forgiveness, of unmerited love, of pardoning mercy? Believe in the Lord Jesus Christ, and you shall be saved. In the day you believe, you shall surely live. You shall be restored to the favor of God, and in His presence is life. You shall be saved from the curse and from the wrath of God. You shall be quickened from the death of sin into the life of righteousness. And if you endure to the end, believing in Jesus, you shall never taste the second death. Having suffered with your Lord, you shall also live and reign with Him forever and ever.

Now this grace is easy to obtain. This condition of life is plain, easy, always at hand. It is in your mouth and in your heart through the operation of the Spirit of God. The moment you believe in your heart in Him whom God has raised from the dead, and confess with your mouth the Lord Jesus as your Lord and your God, you shall be saved from condemnation, from the guilt and punishment of your former sins, and shall have power to serve God in true holiness all the remaining days of your life.

Comparing the Covenants

What is the difference, then, between the righteousness that is of the law and the righteousness that is of faith— between the first covenant (the covenant of works) and the second (the covenant of grace)? The essential, unchangeable difference is this. The one supposes he has already been given to be holy and happy, created in the image and enjoying the favor of God, and prescribes the condition on which he may continue in it, in love and joy, life and immortality. The other knows himself to be unholy and unhappy, fallen short of the glorious image of God, having the wrath of God abiding on him, and hastening through sin, through which his soul is dead, to bodily death, and finally death everlasting. To the man in this state, it prescribes the condition on which he may regain the treasure he has lost, to recover the favor and image of God, retrieve the life of God in his soul, and be restored to the knowledge and the love of God, which is the beginning of eternal life.

Simply, the covenant of works, in order for man to continue in the favor of God, in His knowledge and love, in holiness and happiness, requires of perfect man a perfect and uninterrupted obedience to every point of the law of God. On the other hand, the covenant of grace allows one to recover the favor and the life of God. It requires only a living faith in Jesus, who, through God, justifies all who do not obey.

To repeat, the covenant of works required Adam and all his children to pay the price themselves, in consideration of which they were to receive all the future blessings of God. But, in the covenant of grace, since we have nothing to pay, God forgives us all, provided only that we believe in Jesus, who paid the price for us by giving himself as an atoning sacrifice for our sins.

In this manner, the first covenant required what is now far away from all the children of men, namely, unsinning obedience—something unattainable for those who are conceived and born in sin. But the second requires what is nearby, as if it would say, "You are sin. God is love. You, by sin, have fallen short of the glory of God, yet there is mercy with Him. So bring all your sins to the pardoning God, and they will vanish away as a mist. If you were godly, there would be no cause for Him to justify you as ungodly. But now, draw near in full assurance of faith. Christ speaks and it is done. Fear not, only believe, for the just God justifies all who believe in Jesus."

These things considered, it will be easy to show the folly of trusting in the righteousness of works, which is of the law, and the wisdom of submitting to the righteousness that is of faith.

The folly of those who still trust in the righteousness of the law, doing works to live, is that they set out wrong; therefore, their very first step is a fundamental mistake. Before they can ever think of claiming any blessing from this covenant, they must suppose themselves to be in the same state as those to whom this covenant was made. How vain this supposition is since it was made with Adam, who was in a state of innocence. How foolish are those who thus build on such a weak foundation, never considering that the covenant of works was not given to man when he was dead in trespasses and sins but when he was alive to God, when he knew no sin but was holy as God is holy. They forget that the covenant with Adam was never designed for the recovery of favor and life of God, once lost, but only for the continuance and increase thereof till it becomes complete in life everlasting.

Neither do those who are seeking to establish their own righteousness consider what manner of obedience or righteousness the law indispensably requires. That obedience must be perfect and entire in *every* point or it does not answer the demands of the law. But who is able to perform such obedience, or, consequently, to live in this manner? Who among you fulfills every jot and tittle, even of the outward commandments of God, doing nothing, great or small, which God forbids? Who leaves nothing undone that He orders, or speaks no idle word? Does your conversation always minister grace to the hearers? Whether you eat or drink, or whatever you do, is it all to the glory of God?

How much less are you able to fulfill all the inward commandments of God, those that require every temper and emotion of your soul to be holiness to the Lord. Are you able to love God with all your heart? To love mankind as your own soul? To pray without ceasing? In everything to give thanks? To have God always before you? To keep every affection, desire, and thought in obedience to His law?

You should further consider that the righteousness of the law requires not only obeying every command of God, negative and positive, internal and external, but also obeying perfectly and absolutely. In every instance, whatever the voice of the law is, you must serve the Lord your God with all your strength. It allows no decrease of any kind, it excuses no defect. It condemns every coming short of the full measure of obedience, and immediately pronounces a curse on the offender. It regards only the invariable rules of justice, and says, "I show no mercy."

Who, then, can appear before such a Judge, who unmercifully notes what is done wrong? How weak are they who desire to be tried at the bar, where no living person can be justified? None of the offspring of Adam. For, suppose we did keep every commandment with all our strength, yet one single breach, whatever it might be, destroys our whole claim to life. If we have ever offended in any one point, our righteousness is at an end, for the law condemns all who do not perform uninterrupted as well as perfect obedience. So, anyone who has sinned once, in any degree, faces only a future fiery indignation that shall devour lawbreakers as the adversaries of God.

Is it not, then, the very foolishness of folly for fallen man, shaped in wickedness and conceived in sin, to seek life by this righteousness? By nature, man is earthly, sensual, devilish, altogether corrupt and abominable. In him, until he finds grace, no good thing dwells. He cannot, by himself, think one good thought. He is indeed all sin, a mere lump of ungodliness. He commits sin in every breath he draws. His actual transgressions, in word and deed, are more numerous than the hairs on his head. What stupidity, what senselessness it is for such an unclean, guilty, helpless sinner such as this to dream of seeking acceptance by "his own righteousness," of living by the righteousness that is of the law.

All the arguments that prove the folly of trusting in the righteousness of the law prove equally the wisdom of submitting by faith to the righteousness of God. It is of utmost importance to set aside any claims of our own righteousness. We must acknowledge with our heart, as well as lips, our true state. We must recognize and acknowledge that we bring with us into the world a corrupt sinful nature—more corrupt, indeed, than we can fully or easily conceive or find words to express. We are prone to all that is evil, and averse from all that is good. We are full of pride, self-will, unruly passions, foolish desires, vile and inordinate affections, and love the world more than God.

Our lives have been no better than our hearts. We are

ungodly and unholy in many ways, so much so that our actual sins, both in word and deed, have been as numerous as the stars. On all these accounts, we are displeasing to Him who is of purer eyes than to behold iniquity, and deserve nothing from Him but indignation, wrath, and death, the due wages of sin. We cannot, by any of our righteousness—for indeed we have none—nor by any of our works appease the wrath of God or avert the punishment we have justly deserved. If left to ourselves, we shall only become worse and worse, sink deeper and deeper into sin, and offend God more and more, both with our evil works and with the evil tempers of our carnal mind, until we complete the measure of our iniquities and bring on ourselves swift destruction. Is this not our natural state? An act of true wisdom, then is to acknowledge this with our hearts and lips, and disclaim any righteousness under the law, being honest about the real nature of things.

The wisdom of submitting to the righteousness of faith appears from this consideration that it is the righteousness of God. It is the method of reconciliation with God that has been chosen and established by God himself, not only as He is the God of wisdom, but as He is the sovereign Lord of heaven and earth, and of every creature He has made. It is true wisdom, it is a mark of sound understanding to agree with whatever He has chosen, to say in this, as in all things, "It is the Lord. Let Him do what seems good to Him."

Consider further that it was of mere grace, of free love, of undeserved mercy, that God has given to sinful man any way of reconciliation with himself, that we were not cut away from His hand and utterly blotted out of His remembrance. It is wise to accept whatever method He is pleased to appoint through His tender mercy and unmerited goodness, whereby we, His enemies who have so deeply revolted from Him and so long and obstinately rebelled against Him, may still find favor in His sight.

Let me mention one more consideration. It is wisdom to aim at the best end by the best means. Now, the best end any creature can pursue is happiness in God. The best end a fallen creature can pursue is the recovery of the favor and image of God. But the best, indeed the only means under heaven given to man, whereby he may regain the favor of God, or the image of God, is submitting to the righteousness that is of faith and believing in Jesus.

Whoever you are, therefore, who desire to be forgiven and reconciled to the favor of God, do not say in your heart, "I must first conquer every sin, break off every evil word and work, and do all good to all men. Or I must first go to church, receive the Lord's supper, hear more sermons, and say more prayers." Alas, you are lost from the way. You are still ignorant of the righteousness of God, and are seeking to establish your own righteousness as the hope of your reconciliation. Do you not know that you can do nothing but sin till you are reconciled to God? Why, then, do you say, I must do this and this first, and then I shall believe. No! First believe! Believe in the Lord Jesus Christ, the atoning sacrifice for your sins. Let this good foundation be laid first, and then you shall do all things well.

Never say in your heart, I cannot be accepted yet because I am not good enough. Who is good enough, who ever was, to merit acceptance at God's hands? Was ever any child of Adam good enough for this, or will any be good enough, till the end of all things? As for you, you are not good at all, for there dwells in you no good thing. You never will be until you believe in Jesus. Rather, you will find yourself worse and worse. But there is no need to be worse in order to be accepted. Are you not bad enough already? Indeed you are, and God knows it. Do not deny it, do not delay. All things are now ready. Arise, and wash away your sins. The fountain is open. Now is the time to wash yourself white in the blood of the Lamb. Now He will purge you, and you shall be clean. He will wash you and you will be whiter than snow. Do not say, I am not contrite enough, I am not enough aware of my sins. I know it. I wish to God you were more aware of them and a thousand times more contrite than you are. But do not hold back for this reason. It may be God will make you so, not before you believe, but by believing. It may be you will not weep much until you love much because you have had much forgiven.

In the meantime, look to Jesus. Behold, how He loves you. What more could He have done for you that He has not done? Look steadily upon Him until He looks on you and breaks your hard heart. Then will your head be waters and your eyes fountains of tears. Do not say, I must do something more before I come to Christ. I grant, supposing your Lord should delay His coming, it is right to wait for His appearing in doing, so far as you are able, whatever He has commanded you. But there is no necessity for making such a supposition. How do you know He will delay? Perhaps He will appear, as the dayspring from on high, before the morning light. Do not set Him a time, but expect Him every hour. Now he is near, even at the door!

What reason have you to wait for more sincerity before your sins are blotted out to make you more worthy of the grace of God? Alas, you are still trying to establish your own righteousness. He will have mercy, not because you are worthy of it, but because His compassions do not fail; not because you are righteous, but because Jesus Christ has atoned for your sins.

Again, if there is anything good in sincerity, why do you expect it before you have faith? Faith itself is the only root of whatever is really good and holy.

Above all, how long will you forget that whatever you do or whatever you have before your sins are forgiven is worth nothing with God toward the procuring of your forgiveness? It must all be cast behind your back, trampled underfoot, made no account of, or you will never find favor in God's sight. Until then, you cannot ask it, as a mere sinner, guilty, lost, undone, having nothing to plead, nothing to offer to God, but only the merits of His well-beloved Son, who loved you and gave himself for you.

Whoever you are, who has the sentence of death in yourself, who feels yourself a condemned sinner, and has the wrath of God abiding on you, unto you the Lord does not say, "Do this, perfectly obey all my commands, and live," but, "Believe on the Lord Jesus Christ, and thou shalt be saved." The word of faith is near you. Now, at this instant—in the present moment and in your present state—sinner that you are, just as you are, believe the gospel, and "I will be merciful unto thy unrighteousness, and thy iniquities will I remember no more."

7

The Witness of the Spirit

The Spirit itself beareth witness with our spirit, that we are the children of God. (Romans 8:16)

No one who believes the Scriptures to be God's Word can doubt the importance of this truth. This truth is revealed not only once—neither obscurely nor incidentally—but frequently, in express terms, solemnly and with set purpose, as setting forth one of the peculiar privileges of the children of God.

It is necessary to explain and defend this truth against two specific dangers. *If we deny it*, there is a danger our religion might degenerate into mere formality. Then, having only a form of godliness, we might neglect, if not deny, the power of it. *If we accept it*, but do not fully understand it, we might run into all the wildness of fanaticism. It is necessary, therefore, in every way, to guard against both these dangers through a scriptural and rational illustration and confirmation of this wonderful truth.

It may seem something of this kind is more necessary because so little has been written clearly on the subject, except for a few speeches on the wrong side of the question that

Taken from John Wesley's, *Sermons on Several Occasions*, "The Witness of the Spirit, Discourse II," XI, Vol. 1, p. 93ff.

attempt to explain it away. Doubtless these were caused, at least in a great part, by crude, unscriptural, irrational interpretations by some who did not understand the experience.

Christians should understand, explain, and defend this doctrine, because it is a principal part of the testimony that God has given us to bear to all mankind. It is by His special blessing upon them in searching the Scriptures, confirmed by the experience of His children, that this great evangelical truth has been recovered.

But what is the witness of the Spirit? The original Greek word may be translated either, as it is in several places, "the witness," or, less ambiguously, "the testimony" or "the record." It is translated this way in 1 John 5:11: "This is the record, that God hath given to us eternal life, and this life is in his Son." The testimony now under consideration is given by the Spirit of God to and with our spirit. He is the person testifying. He testifies to us that we are the children of God. The immediate result of this testimony is the fruit of the Spirit—love, joy, peace, longsuffering, gentleness, goodness. Without these, the testimony itself cannot continue. It is inevitably destroyed, not only by the commission of any outward sin, or the omission of known duty, but also by giving way to any inward sin. In a word, it can be destroyed by whatever grieves the Holy Spirit of God.

It is hard to find words in human language to explain the deep things of God. Indeed there are no words to adequately express what the Spirit of God works in His children. By the Spirit I mean an inward impression on the soul, whereby the Spirit of God immediately and directly witnesses to my spirit that I am a child of God; that Jesus Christ has loved me and given himself for me; that all my sins are blotted out, and I, even I, am reconciled to God.

I do not mean that the Spirit of God testifies this by any outward voice, nor always by an inward voice, although He may do this sometimes. Neither do I suppose that He always applies to the heart, though He often may, one or more texts of Scripture. But He works upon the soul by His immediate influence, and by a strong, though inexplicable operation, in such a way that the stormy wind and troubled waves subside, and there is a sweet calm. The heart rests as if in the arms of Jesus, and the sinner is clearly satisfied that he is reconciled to God, that all his iniquities are forgiven and his sins covered.

What can be disputed about this? There definitely is a witness or testimony of the Spirit with our spirit that we are the children of God. None can deny this without flatly contradicting the Scriptures and charging that God lies. Therefore, that there is a testimony of the Spirit is acknowledged by all parties.

Neither is it questioned whether there is an indirect witness, or testimony, that we are the children of God. This is nearly, if not exactly, the same as the testimony of a good conscience toward God. It is the result of reason, or reflection on what we feel in our own souls. Strictly speaking, it is a conclusion drawn partly from the Word of God and partly from our own experience. The Word of God says everyone who has the fruit of the Spirit is a child of God. Experience, or inward consciousness, tells me that I have the fruit of the Spirit. Therefore, I rationally conclude I am a child of God. This is agreed on everywhere, and so it is not a matter of controversy.

There can be no real testimony of the Spirit without the fruit of the Spirit. We assert that the fruit of the Spirit immediately springs from this testimony, but not always with the same clarity, even when the testimony is first given. And the testimony itself is not always equally strong and clear.

But the point in question is whether there is any direct testimony of the Spirit at all, or whether there is any testimony of the Spirit other than that which arises from an awareness of the fruit. I believe there is, because that is the plain, natural meaning of the text, "The Spirit itself beareth witness with our spirit, that we are the children of God." It is evident there are two witnesses mentioned who together testify the same thing: the Spirit of God and our own spirit. When our spirit is conscious of love, joy, peace, longsuffering, gentleness, and goodness, it easily concludes from this that we are the children of God.

It is true that some suppose the other witness to be self-consciousness of our own good works. This, they believe, is the testimony of God's Spirit. But this is actually still part of the testimony of our own spirit. As Paul said, this is our boast, our conscience testifying that we have conducted ourselves in the world in the holiness, simplicity, and sincerity that are from God. This refers to our words and actions at least as much as to our inward dispositions. So this is not another witness, but the very same witness of our own spirit that he mentioned before. The consciousness of our good works is only one element of it. Consequently here is only one witness still.

If the text speaks of two witnesses, therefore, one of these is not the consciousness of our good works. All this is contained in the witness of our spirit. What then is the other witness? This might easily be learned, if the text itself were not sufficiently clear, from the verse immediately preceding: "Ye have not received the spirit of bondage . . . [but] the spirit of adoption, whereby we cry, Abba, Father." It follows, "The Spirit itself beareth witness with our spirit, that we are the children of God."

This is further explained by the parallel text in Gal. 4:6: "Because ye are sons, God hath sent forth the Spirit of his Son into your hearts, crying, Abba, Father." This is something immediate and direct, not the result of meditation or reasoning. This Spirit cries, "Abba, Father," in our hearts the moment it is given, prior to any thought about our sincerity, or to any reasoning at all. This is the plain natural meaning of Paul's words, which strikes anyone as soon as he hears them. All these texts, in their most obvious meaning, describe a direct testimony of the Spirit.

The Need for the Spirit's Direct Witness

That the testimony of the Spirit of God must, in the very nature of things, come before the testimony of our own spirit, appears from this single consideration. We must be holy in heart and life before we can be conscious that we are so. But we must love God *before* we can be holy at all, this being the root of all holiness. We cannot love God until we know He loves us. We love Him because He first loved us, and we cannot know His love to us until His Spirit witnesses it to our spirit. Until then we cannot believe it, we cannot say, "The life which I now live in the flesh I live by the faith of the Son of God, who loved me and gave himself for me" (Gal.2:20). Since, therefore, the testimony of His Spirit must precede the love of God, and all holiness, then it must precede our consciousness of it.

To confirm this scriptural doctrine, we have the experience of the children of God, the experience not of two or three, not of a few, but of a great multitude. It has been confirmed, both in this and in all ages, by clouds of witnesses. It is confirmed by your experience and mine. The Spirit himself bore witness to my spirit that I was a child of God, gave me an evidence of it, and I immediately cried, "Abba, Father!" This I did before I reflected on, or was conscious of, any fruit of the Spirit. It was from this testimony received that love, joy, peace, and the whole fruit of the Spirit flowed.

But this is confirmed not only by the experience of the children of God (thousands of whom can declare that they never did know themselves to be in the favor of God until it was directly witnessed to them by His Spirit) but by all those who are convinced of sin, who feel the wrath of God abiding on them. These cannot be satisfied with anything less than a direct testimony from His Spirit that He is merciful to their unrighteousness and remembers their sins and iniquities no more. Tell any of these, "You are to know you are a child of God, by reflecting on what He has worked in you, on your love, joy, and peace." You will receive the immediate reply,

"By all this I know I am a child of the devil. I have no more love to God than the devil has. My carnal mind is against God. I have no joy in the Holy Spirit. My soul is sorrowful even unto death. I have no peace. My mind is a troubled sea, I am all storm and tempest."

How can such souls possibly be comforted except by a divine testimony—not of their goodness, sincerity, or conformity to the Scripture in heart and life, but to the fact that God justifies the ungodly. God justifies him who, until the moment he is justified, is all ungodly, void of all true holiness. Justification comes to him who works nothing that is truly good until he is conscious that he is accepted not for any works of righteousness he has done but by the pure, free mercy of God—wholly and solely for what the Son of God has done and suffered for us. It cannot be otherwise if a man is justified by faith without the works of the law.

What inward or outward goodness can he be conscious of prior to his justification? Being conscious that there dwells in him no good thing, neither inward nor outward goodness, is essentially, indispensably necessary before he can be justified freely through the redemption that is in Jesus Christ. No one was ever justified, nor can any man ever be justified until he is brought to that point of knowledge of his own worthlessness in order to give up all to God. Everyone who denies the existence of such a testimony does in effect deny justification by faith. It follows that either he has never experienced this (he was never justified), or he has forgotten, as Peter says, the purification from his former sins. He has forgotten the experience he himself then had, the manner in which God worked in his own soul when his former sins were blotted out.

The experience even of non-Christians here confirms that of those reborn of God. Many of them have a desire to please God. Some of them take great pains to please Him, but they consider it the height of absurdity for anyone to talk of knowing his sins are forgiven. All of them even deny the existence of such a thing. Yet many of them are conscious of their own sincerity. Many of them undoubtedly have, in a degree, the testimony of their own spirit, a consciousness of their own uprightness. But this brings them no consciousness that they are forgiven, no knowledge that they are accepted by God. The more sincere they are, the more uneasy they generally are for lack of assurance. This plainly shows that it cannot be known, in a satisfactory manner, by the bare testimony of our own spirit without God's directly testifying that we are His children.

Many objections have been made to the testimony that we can know we are forgiven. The main one is next considered.

It is objected, "Experience is not sufficient to prove a doctrine that is not founded on Scripture." This is an important truth, but it does not affect the present question because the doctrine before us is founded on Scripture. Therefore, experience is properly included in confirmation of it.

"But madmen, pseudo-prophets, and fanatics of every kind have imagined they experienced God's present witness." They have, and perhaps not a few of them did, although they did not retain the witness long. But if they did not, this is no proof at all that others have not experienced it. A madman's imagining himself a king does not prove that there are no real kings.

"Many who have pleaded strongly for this have utterly denied the Bible." Perhaps so, but this was not a necessary consequence. Thousands plead for it who have the highest esteem for the Bible.

It is further objected, "The purpose of the witness is to prove the profession we make is genuine, and this does not provide proof."

I answer, proving is not the purpose. His witness is prior to our making any profession at all except that of being lost, undone, guilty, helpless sinners. It is designed to assure those to whom it is given that they are the children of God, that they are justified freely by His grace through redemption in Jesus Christ. This does not suppose that their preceding thoughts, words, and actions are conformable to any rule of Scripture. It supposes quite the opposite, namely, that they are sinners all over, both in heart and life. If it were otherwise, God would justify the ungodly, and their own works would be counted to them for righteousness.

It appears that a supposition of being justified by works is at the root of all these objections. Whoever heartily believes that God attributes to all who are justified righteousness without works will find no difficulty in agreeing that the witness of His Spirit precedes the fruit of it.

Yet another objection is, "The Scripture says, 'The tree is known by its fruits. Prove all things. Try the spirits. Examine yourselves.' " Most true. Therefore, let every man who believes he has the witness in himself try whether it be of God. If good fruit follows, it is; otherwise it is not. Certainly the tree is known by its fruit, and by that fruit we prove if it is of God. But the direct witness is never referred to alone in the book of God. It does not stand alone as a single witness, but is connected with the other, as giving a joint testimony, testifying with our spirit that we are children of God.

If you think otherwise, examine yourself as to whether you are in the faith and prove yourself. Do you not know that Jesus Christ is in you? Is it not clear that this is known by direct as well as a remote witness? How is it proved that others did not know it—first, by an inward consciousness, and next by love, joy, and peace? "But the testimony arising from the internal and external change is constantly referred to in the Bible." That is so, and we constantly state this, to confirm the testimony of the Spirit. "All the evidence you have given, to distinguish the operations of God's Spirit from delusion, refer to the change wrought in us and upon us." Yes, this is undoubtedly true.

Some object, "The direct witness of the Spirit alone does not keep us from the greatest delusion. So can the direct witness—whose testimony cannot be depended on alone—be trusted when it is forced to use something more to prove what it asserts, namely, the witness of our spirits?"

I answer, to secure us from all delusion, God gives us two witnesses that we are His children; they testify together. Therefore, what God has joined together, let man not tear apart. While they are joined, we cannot be deluded. Their testimony can be depended on. They are fit to be trusted to the highest degree, and need nothing else to prove what they assert.

The direct witness only asserts; it does not prove anything. But by two witnesses shall every word be established. And when the Spirit witnesses with our spirit, as God designs Him to do, then it fully proves that we are children of God.

Another objection is, "You say the change made is a sufficient testimony unless in the case of severe trials, such as that of our Savior on the cross, but none of us can be tried in that manner." You or I may be tried in such a manner, and so may any other child of God, so it will be impossible for us to keep our filial confidence in God without the direct witness of His Spirit.

A final objection is, "The greatest contenders for His witness are some of the proudest and most uncharitable of men." Perhaps some of the hottest contenders for it are both proud and uncharitable, but some of the firmest contenders for it are eminently meek and lowly in heart.

The preceding objections are the strongest I have heard. Yet I believe whoever calmly and impartially considers those objections and the answers together will easily see that they do not destroy, or weaken, the evidence of that great truth, that the Spirit of God does directly, as well as indirectly, testify that we are children of God.

To sum this up, the testimony of the Spirit is an inward impression on the souls of belivers, whereby God directly testifies to their spirit that they are children of God. The question is not whether there is a testimony of the Spirit, but whether there is any direct testimony, whether there is any other than that which arises from a consciousness of the fruit of the Spirit. I believe there is. This is the plain natural meaning of the text, illustrated both by the preceding words and the parallel passage in the letter to the Galatians. In the nature of it, the testimony must precede the fruit that then springs forth. This plain meaning of the Word of God is confirmed by the experience of innumerable Christians, by all who are convicted of sin, who can never rest till they have a direct witness, and even of the children of the world, who, not having the witness in themselves, declare no one can know his sins are forgiven.

Let me answer all objections.

"Experience is not sufficient to prove a doctrine unsupported by Scripture." Experience is sufficient to confirm a doctrine that is grounded on Scripture.

"Madmen and zealots of every kind have imagined such a witness." Though many fancy they experience what they do not, this is not prejudicial to real experience.

"The purpose of that witness is to prove our profession genuine, which design it does not answer." The purpose of that witness is to assure us we are children of God, and this purpose it does answer.

"Scripture says the tree is known by its fruit; examine yourselves; prove your own selves, and meantime, the direct witness is never referred to in all the book of God." The true witness of the Spirit is known by its fruit—love, peace, and joy. These do not come before the witness, but follow it.

"It cannot be proved that the direct, as well as the indirect, witness is referred to in that very text: 'Know ye not your own selves how that Jesus Christ is in you?' (2 Cor. 13:5). Therefore, it does not secure us from the greatest delusions." The Spirit of God, witnessing with our spirit, does secure us from all delusion.

"The change wrought in us is a sufficient testimony, unless in such trials as Jesus alone suffered." We are all liable to trials, in which the testimony of our own spirit is not sufficient, in which nothing but the direct testimony of God's Spirit can assure us that we are His children.

Two inferences may be drawn from all this. First, let no

one ever presume to rest on any testimony that separates the Spirit from its fruit. If the Spirit of God does really testify that we are children of God, the immediate consequence will be the fruit of the Spirit—love, joy, peace, longsuffering, gentleness, goodness, faith, meekness, temperance. This fruit may be clouded for a while, however, during a time of strong temptation. Then it does not appear to the tempted person while Satan is buffeting him, yet the substantial part of it remains, even in the darkest times. It is true that joy in the Holy Spirit may be missing during a time of trial. The soul may be terribly sorrowful while the time and power of darkness continue, but even this is generally restored with increase until we again rejoice with joy unspeakable and full of glory.

The second inference is this. Let none rest in any supposed fruit of the Spirit without the witness. There may be foretastes of joy, of peace, of love, and those are not deceptive, but really from God, long before we have the witness in ourselves. They may come even before the Spirit of God witnesses with our spirits that we have redemption in the blood of Jesus, even our forgiveness of sins. There may be a degree of longsuffering, of gentleness, of faith, meekness, and temperance. Not a shadow, but a real measure, by God's grace in allowing it before we are accepted in the Beloved, before we have a testimony of our acceptance. Yet, one should never be satisfied by this. It is at the peril of our souls if we do. If we are wise, we shall be continually crying to God until His Spirit cries in our heart, "Abba, Father!" This is the gift and assurance known by all the children of God. Without this we can never be assured that we are His children. Without this we cannot retain a steady peace or avoid perplexing doubts and fears. Once we have received this Spirit of adoption, the peace that passes all understanding and expels all painful doubt and fear will keep our hearts and minds in Christ Jesus. It is undoubtedly the will of God, who calls us, to give us again what He has once given. This grace is given so that no one need ever be deprived of either the testimony of God's Spirit or the testimony of our own—the consciousness of our walking in all righteousness and true holiness.

8

The Wilderness State

Ye now therefore have sorrow: but I will see you again, and your heart shall rejoice, and your joy no man taketh from you. (John 16:22)

After God had worked a great deliverance for Israel by bringing them out of the house of bondage, they did not immediately enter into the land He had promised to their fathers. They wandered out of the way in the wilderness, and were variously tempted and distressed. In like manner, after God has delivered Christians from the bondage of sin and Satan, when they are justified freely by His grace through the redemption that is in Jesus, not many immediately enter into the peace and rest that remains for His people. Most of them wander, more or less, out of the good path into which He has brought them. They come, as it were, into a vast and howling spiritual desert, where they are variously tempted and tormented. In allusion to the experience of the Israelites, some have termed this "a wilderness state."

It is certain those in that condition deserve the tenderest compassion. They labor under an evil and sore distress, though one that is not commonly understood. For this very

---

Taken from John Wesley's, *Sermons on Several Occasions*, "The Wilderness State," XLVI, Vol. 1, p. 408 ff.

reason it is more difficult for them to find a remedy. Being in darkness themselves, they cannot be supposed to understand the nature of their own disorder. Few of their brothers or sisters, or perhaps even their teachers, know either what their sickness is or how to heal it. This makes it all the more important to inquire about the nature of this disease, its cause, and its cure.

First, what is the nature of this disease into which so many fall after they have believed? Of what does it consist, and what are the genuine symptoms of it? It consists in the loss of that faith which God once worked in their heart. Those who are in the wilderness do not now have that inward demonstration of the Spirit that previously enabled each of them to say, "The life which I now live in the flesh I live by the faith of the Son of God, who loved me, and gave himself for me" (Gal. 2:20).

The light of heaven does not now shine in their hearts, and they do not experience Him who is invisible. Darkness is again on the face of their souls and blindness on the eyes of their understanding. The Spirit no longer witnesses with their spirits that they are the children of God, nor does He continue as the spirit of adoption, crying in their hearts, "Abba, Father." They now do not have a sure trust in His love and a liberty of approaching Him with holy boldness. "Though he slay me, yet will I trust in him" (Job 13:15) is no longer the language of their heart. They are shorn of their strength, and become weak and spiritually feeble, just as the unsaved.

Next comes the loss of love, which can only rise or fall at the same time and in the same proportion with true, living faith. Accordingly, those who are deprived of their faith are also deprived of the love of God. They cannot now say, "Lord, you know all things. You know that I love you." They are not now happy in God, as everyone is who truly loves Him. They do not delight in Him as in times past, or smell the perfume of His presence. Once all their desire was for Him, to the remembrance of His name. Now even their desires are cold and dead, if not utterly extinguished.

As their love of God has grown cold, so also has their love of their neighbor. They don't have that zeal for the souls of men, that longing after their welfare, that fervent, restless, active desire of being reconciled to God. They do not feel the heart of mercy for the sheep who are lost, that tender compassion for the ignorant and those who are out of the way. Once they were gentle toward all men, meekly instructing those who opposed the truth. If one was overtaken in a fault, they restored such a person in the spirit of meekness; but now meekness is disappearing and anger is beginning to regain its power. Peevishness and impatience attack them to make them fall, or sometimes even drive them to render evil for evil and insult for insult.

In consequence of the loss of faith and love, next follows loss of joy in the Holy Spirit. If the loving consciousness of pardon is gone, the joy resulting from it cannot remain. If the Spirit does not witness with our spirit that we are the children of God, the joy that flowed from the inward witness must also be at an end. And, likewise, they who once rejoiced with joy unspeakable, in hope of the glory of God, are now deprived of that hope of immortality. Now they are deprived of the joy it brought, as well as a consciousness of the love of God, which once had filled their hearts. For when the cause is removed, so is the effect. When the fountain is dammed up, those living waters spring no more to refresh the thirsty soul.

With the loss of faith, love, and joy, there is also the loss of that peace which once passed all understanding. That sweet tranquillity of mind, that composure of spirit is gone. Painful doubt returns—doubt whether we ever did, and perhaps whether we ever shall, believe. We begin to doubt whether we ever did find in our hearts the real testimony of the Spirit. We begin to wonder whether we deceived our own souls, and mistook the voice of nature for the voice of God. We even doubt whether we shall ever hear His voice and find favor in His sight. These doubts are again joined with fear, a fear that has torment. We fear the wrath of God even as before we believed. We fear lest we should be cast out of His presence, and then sink again into that fear of death, from which we had been wholly delivered.

But even this is not all, for loss of peace is accompanied by loss of power. We know everyone who has peace with God through Jesus Christ has power over all sin. While our peace remained, power also remained, even over the most besetting sin, whether it was the sin of his nature, his constitution, his education, his profession, even over those evil tempers and desires which, till then, he could not conquer. Sin had then no more dominion over him, but he now has no more dominion over sin. He may struggle still, but he cannot overcome. The crown has fallen from his head. His enemies again prevail over him, and more or less bring him into bondage. The glory has departed from him, even the kingdom of God which was in his heart. He is dispossessed of righteousness as well as of peace and joy in the Holy Spirit.

Such is the nature of what many have termed "The wilderness state." But the nature of it may be more fully understood by inquiring, What are the causes of it? These, indeed, are diverse. But I dare not rank among those who are walking in it. God rejoices in the prosperity of His servants. He has no delight in the afflictions or griefs of His children. His invariable will is our sanctification, attended by peace and joy in the Holy Spirit. These are His own free gifts, and we are assured the gifts of God are, on His part, without repentance. He never repents of what He has given, or desires to withdraw them from us. Therefore He never deserts us, as some say; it is only we who desert Him.

The Source of the Problem

The most usual cause of inward darkness is sin of one kind or another. It is this which generally brings on what is often a complication of sin and misery.

First is the sin of commission. This may frequently be

observed to darken the soul in a moment, especially if it is a known, willful, or presumptuous sin. If, for instance, a person who is now walking in the clear light of God's countenance should be in any way prevailed on to commit a single act of drunkenness or uncleanness, it would be no wonder if, in that very hour, he fell into utter darkness. It is true, there have been some very rare cases in which God has prevented this, by an extraordinary display of His pardoning mercy, almost in the very instant. But in general, such an abuse of the goodness of God, so gross an insult on His love, causes an immediate estrangement from God and a darkness that may be felt.

But it may be hoped this does not occur often, or that there are none who so despise the riches of His goodness that they rebel against Him grossly while they walk in His light.

However, the soul's light is much more frequently lost by giving way to sins of omission. This, indeed, does not quench the Spirit immediately, but gradually and slowly. The former may be compared to pouring water upon a fire, the latter to withdrawing the fuel from it. Many times that loving Spirit will reprove our neglect before He departs from us. Many are the inward checks, the secret notices He gives, before His influences are withdrawn. Only a train of omissions, willfully persisted in, can bring us into utter darkness.

Perhaps no sin of omission more frequently causes this than the neglect of private prayer. The lack of this cannot be supplied by any other means whatever. Nothing can be more plain than that the life of God in the soul does not continue, much less increase, unless we use all opportunities to pour out our hearts to Him. If, therefore, we are negligent of this, if we allow business, company, or any avocation whatever, to prevent these secret exercises of the soul, or to make us hurry over them in a slight and careless manner, that life will surely decay. If we allow them to be interrupted frequently, or sometimes omit them, it will gradually die away.

Another sin of omission that frequently brings the soul of a believer into darkness is the neglect of what was so strongly commanded, even under the Jewish dispensation. Rebuke your neighbor frankly so you will not share in his guilt, but never hate your brother in your heart. Now, if we hate our brother in our heart, or do not rebuke him when we see him in a fault, poverty will soon seep into our own soul, and we become partakers of his sin. By neglecting to reprove our neighbor, we make his sin our own. We become accountable for it to God. We saw his danger and gave him no warning, so, if he perishes in his iniquity, God may justly require his blood at our hands. No wonder, then, if by thus grieving the Spirit, we lose His presence.

Another cause of our losing this is giving way to some kind of inward sin. For example, we know everyone who is proud of heart is an abomination to the Lord, even though this pride of heart does not appear in our outward conversation. How easily a soul, filled with joy and peace, may fall into the snare of the devil. How natural it is for him to imagine that he has more grace, more wisdom, or strength than he really has, to think more highly of himself than he ought to think. How natural to glory in something he has been given as if he had earned it. But since God continually resists the proud, and gives grace only to the humble, this must certainly obscure, if not wholly destroy, the light that previously shone in his heart.

The same effect may be produced by giving in to anger, whatever the provocation or occasion, even though it might be called zeal for the truth or for the glory of God. Indeed, all zeal that is anything but love is earthly, animal, and devilish. It is the flame of wrath, it is flat, sinful anger, neither better nor worse. Nothing is a greater enemy to the gentle love of God than this. Love and anger never did, and never can, subsist together in one heart. In the same proportion as this prevails, love and joy in the Holy Spirit decrease. This is particularly observable in the case of offense. By this I mean anger at any of our brothers or sisters, at any of those who are united with us either by civil or religious ties. If we give way to the spirit of offense but one moment, we lose the sweet influences of the Holy Spirit, so that, instead of amending them, we destroy ourselves and become an easy prey to any enemy that assaults us.

But even if we are aware of this snare of the devil, we may be attacked from another quarter. When fierceness and anger are asleep, and love alone is waking, we may be no less endangered by desire, which equally tends to darken the soul. This is the sure effect of any foolish desire, any vain or inordinate affection. If we set our affection on things of the earth, on any person or thing under the sun, if we desire anything but God and what inclines to God, if we seek happiness in any creature, the jealous God will surely contend with us, for He will admit to no rival. If we will not hear His warning voice and return to Him with our whole soul, if we continue to grieve Him with our idols, and run after other gods, we shall soon be cold, barren, and dry, and the god of this world will blind and darken our hearts.

This he frequently does, even when we do not give way to any positive sin. It is enough to give him sufficient advantage if we do not stir up the gift of God that is in us, if we do not agonize continually to enter in at the narrow gate, if we do not strive for the mastery and take the kingdom of heaven by storm. If we do not fight, we are sure to be conquered. Let us only be careless or faint in our mind, let us be easy and indolent, and our natural darkness will soon return and overspread our soul. Therefore, if we give way to spiritual sloth, this will effectually darken the soul. It will as surely destroy the light of God, though not so swiftly as murder or adultery.

We need to know the cause of our darkness. Whatever it is, whether omission or commission, whether inward or outward sin, is not always easily seen. Sometimes the sin that caused the present distress may lie at a great distance. It might have been committed days, or weeks, or months before. That God now withdraws His light and peace because of what was done so long ago is not an instance of His severity, but rather a proof of His longsuffering and tender mercy. He waits a period to allow us to see, acknowledge, and correct what was wrong. Then at length, He shows His displeasure so that He may bring us to repentance.

Another general cause of this darkness is our ignorance, which may be of various kinds. When Christians do not know the Scriptures, they may imagine there are passages either in the Old or New Testament, which assert that all believers, without exception, must sometimes be in darkness. This ignorance will naturally bring upon them the darkness that they expect. This has been a common cause among us. Only a few do not expect it. It is no wonder because they are taught to expect it, and their guides lead them into this way. Not only the mystic writers of the Roman church but many of the most spiritual and experimental of our own denomination lay this down with much assurance as a plain, unquestionable doctrine from Scripture, citing many texts to prove it.

Ignorance also of the work of God in the soul frequently causes this darkness. Men imagine, because they have been taught to, that they are not always to walk in luminous faith, that such illumination is only a lower spiritual gift. They think that as they rise higher, they are to leave those sensible comforts, and to live by blind faith. Faith is blind indeed if it is stripped of love, peace, and joy in the Holy Spirit. They imagine that a state of light and joy is good, but a state of darkness and dryness is better, that it is by these alone we can be purified from pride, love of the world, and excessive self-love. Therefore, they further imagine, we ought neither to expect nor desire always to walk in the light. So it is, though there may be additional reasons, that the main body of pious men in the early church generally walked in a dark, uncomfortable way, and, if they ever received God's light, soon lost it.

Another general cause of spiritual darkness is temptation. When the grace of the Lord first renews our soul, temptation frequently flees away and totally disappears. All is calm within—perhaps without, too—while God makes our enemies to be at peace with us. It is then very natural to suppose that we shall not see spiritual warfare within us again. There are instances in which this calm has continued, not only for weeks, but for months or years. Usually, however, it is otherwise. In a short time the winds blow, the rains descend, and the floods arise anew. Those who do not know either the Father or the Son, hate Christians, His children. They will show that hatred in various ways when God loosens them from His restraint. Always in the past, he who was born of the flesh persecuted those who were born of the Spirit. It is the same now, with the same cause producing the same effect.

The evil that still remains in the believer's heart will again move, and anger and many other roots of bitterness will strive to spring up. At the same time, Satan will be waiting to cast his fiery darts. Then the Christian soul will have to wrestle not only with the world, not only with flesh and blood, but with principalities and powers, with the rulers of the darkness of this world, with wicked spirits in high places. When so many assaults are made at once, and perhaps with the utmost violence, it is not strange if it should bring on not only heaviness but even darkness in a weak believer. This is especially true if he had foolishly told himself the day of evil would return no more, and he did not watch for or expect these assaults.

The force of those temptations that arise from within will be greatly heightened if we have thought too highly of ourselves, and believed we have been cleansed from all sin.

Naturally we imagine this during the excitement of our first love from God. How ready we are to believe that God has fulfilled in us the whole work of faith with power; and because we feel no sin, we have none in us, and our soul is all love. Well may a sharp attack from a sin we had thought not only conquered but slain throw us into much heaviness of soul or even into utter darkness. Particularly when we reason with this enemy instead of instantly calling upon God, and casting ourselves upon Him, by simple faith, who alone knows how to deliver His children out of temptation.

Finding the Remedy

Understanding the causes of this darkness leaves us with the question, What is the cure?

To suppose the cure is one and the same in all cases is a great and fatal mistake, although it is extremely common, even among many who consider themselves experienced Christians, teachers and spiritual guides of others. Accordingly, they know and use but one medicine, whatever the cause of sickness. They begin immediately to apply the promises, and to preach the gospel, as they call it. Giving comfort is their aim, so they say many soft and tender things concerning the love of God, and the power in the blood of Christ, to poor, helpless sinners. This is quackery of the worst kind, as it tends, except for the mercy of God, to destroy peoples' bodies and souls, sending them to hell.

It is hard to speak of these promise mongers as they deserve. They deserve the title, which has been ignorantly given to others, of "spiritual mountebanks." They, in effect, make the blood of the covenant an unholy thing. They vilely prostitute the promises of God by applying them to all without distinction. In truth, the cure of spiritual, as of bodily diseases, must be as varied as are the causes of them. The first thing is to find out the cause, and this will naturally point out the cure.

For instance, is it sin that causes darkness? If so, which sin? Is it outward sin of any kind? Does your conscience accuse you of committing any sin by which you grieve the Holy Spirit of God? Is it for this reason that He is departed from you, and that joy and peace are departed with Him? How can you expect them to return until you put away that sin? Let the wicked forsake his way. Cleanse your hands, you sinners, and put away the evil of your doings. So shall your light break out of obscurity, and the Lord will return and pardon.

If, after the closest search, you can find no sin of commission that causes the cloud upon your soul, ask next if there is some sin of omission that separates God and you. Do you ignore the sin of your brother? Do you reprove those who sin in your sight? Do you walk in all the commandments of God, in public, family, private prayer? If not, if you habitually neglect any one of these known duties, how can you expect the light of His face to continue shining upon you? Hurry to strengthen the virtues that remain; then your soul shall live. Today if you will hear His voice, by His grace supply what is lacking. When you hear a voice behind you, saying, this is the way, walk in it, do not ignore it. Do not be disobedient to your heavenly calling. Until sin, whether of omission or commission, is removed, all comfort is false and deceitful. It is only bandaging the wound, which still festers and burns. Look for no peace within till you are at peace with God. That cannot be without fruits suitable for repentance.

Perhaps you are not conscious of even any sin of omission that impairs your peace and joy in the Holy Spirit. Is there not, then, some inward sin, which, as a root of bitterness, springs up in your heart to trouble you? Is your dryness, and your barrenness of soul, caused by your heart's departing from the living God? Has the sin of pride come against you? Have you thought of yourself more highly than you ought to think? Have you ascribed your success in any of your undertakings to your own courage, strength, or wisdom? Have you boasted of something God gave you, as though you had earned it? Have you gloried in anything, save in the cross of our Lord Jesus Christ? Have you sought after or desired the praise of men, or have you taken pleasure in it? If so, you see the way you must go. If you have stumbled into pride, humble yourself under the mighty hand of God, and He will exalt you in due time.

Have you forced God to turn from you by giving way to anger? Have you been angered by the ungodly, or been envious of evildoers? Have you been offended at any of your brothers or sisters, looking at their real or imagined sin, thereby sinning yourself against the great law of love by estranging your heart from them? Then look to the Lord to renew your strength, so all this sharpness and coldness may be done away, and that love, and peace, and joy may return together. Then you may be invariably kind to others, tenderhearted, and forgiving, even as God for Christ's sake has forgiven you.

Have you given way to any worldly desire or to any kind or degree of excessive affection? How then can the love of God have a place in your heart until you put away all your earthly idols? Be not deceived, God is not mocked. He will not dwell in a divided heart. As long, therefore, as you cherish a Delilah in your bosom, He has no place there. It is vain to hope for a recovery of His light until you pluck out that desire and cast it away. Let there be no longer any delay. Cry to Him that He may enable you to do so. Admit and lament your own impotence and helplessness. The Lord being your helper, enter in at the narrow gate, and take the kingdom of heaven by storm. Cast out every idol from His sanctuary, and the glory of the Lord will soon appear.

Perhaps it is this very thing, the lack of striving, spiritual sloth, which keeps your soul in darkness. You dwell at ease, with no war in your life, so you are quiet and unconcerned. You go on in the same even track of outward duties, and are content where you are. Do you wonder, in the meantime, that your soul is dead? Stir yourself up before the Lord. Arise, and shake yourself from the dust, wrestle with God for His mighty blessing, pour out your soul to God in prayer, and continue with all perseverance. Awake from sleep, stay awake, and watch. Otherwise, there is nothing to be expected other than you will be alienated more and more from the light and life of God.

If, upon the fullest and most thorough examination of yourself, you do not feel that you at present are subject to spiritual sloth or any inward or outward sin, then call to mind times past. Consider your former tempers, words, and actions. Have these been right before the Lord? Commune with Him in private and be still. Ask Him to search your heart and bring to your memory whatever has at any time offended His eyes. If the guilt of any unrepented sin remains in your soul, you will remain in darkness until, having been renewed by repentance, you are again washed by faith in the fountain opened for sin.

God's cure will be entirely different if the cause of the disease is not sin, but ignorance. It may be ignorance of the meaning of Scripture, perhaps influenced by ignorant commentators. In this case, that ignorance must be removed before we can remove its darkness. We must learn the true meaning of any misundertood texts. We cannot consider all the passages of Scripture that fall into this category. I shall mention only two or three, that are frequently brought to prove that all believers must, sooner or later, walk in darkness.

One of these is Isa. 50:10, "Who is among you that feareth the Lord, that obeyeth the voice of his servant, that walketh in darkness, and hath no light? Let him trust in the name of the Lord, and stay upon his God." But how does it appear, either from the text or context, that the person spoken of here ever had light? We would advise him, though he were still dark of soul and had never seen the light of God's countenance, yet to trust in the name of the Lord and wait upon his God. This text, therefore, does not prove that a believer in Christ must sometimes walk in darkness.

Another text that has been claimed to teach the same doctrine is Hos. 2:14, "I will allure her, and bring her into the wilderness, and speak comfortably unto her." It has been inferred that God will bring every believer into the wilderness, into a state of deadness and darkness. But it is certain the text says no such thing, for it does not appear that it speaks of particular believers at all. It manifestly refers to the Jewish nation, and perhaps only to that. But if it is applicable to particular persons, the plain meaning is this: I will draw him by love, I will next convince him of sin, and then comfort him by my pardoning mercy.

The same inference has been drawn from John 16:22: "Ye now therefore have sorrow: but I will see you again, and your heart shall rejoice, and your joy no man taketh from you." This has been claimed to imply that God would, after a time, withdraw himself from all believers, and that they could not, until after a time of loneliness, have the joy that no man could take from them. The whole context shows that our Lord is here speaking personally to the apostles, and no others. Also, He is speaking about particular events—His own death and resurrection. A little while, He says, and you shall not see me—while I am in the grave. And again, a little while, and you shall see me—when I am risen from the dead (John 16:16). "Ye shall weep and lament, but the world shall rejoice: and ye shall be sorrowful, but your sorrow shall be turned into joy" (John 16:20). All this we know was literally fulfilled in the particular case of the apostles. But no inference can be drawn from this with regard to God's dealings with believers in general.

A fourth and final text, which has been frequently cited to prove the same doctrine, is 1 Pet. 4:12: "Beloved, think it not strange concerning the fiery trial which is to try you." But this is as foreign to the point also. The text, literally translated, says, "Beloved, wonder not at the burning which is among you, which is for your trial." However, this may be accommodated to inward trials in a secondary sense. It primarily refers to martyrdom and the sufferings connected with it. Therefore, this text has nothing in it to prove the point for which it is quoted.

God Cleanses With Light, Not Darkness

Is darkness much more profitable for the soul than light? Is the work of God in the heart most swiftly and effectually carried on during a state of inward suffering? Is a believer more swiftly and thoroughly purified by sorrow than by joy, by anguish and pain and distress and spiritual martyrdoms than by continual peace? The mystics taught this, and wrote it in their books, but it is not in the messages of God. The Scripture nowhere says that the absence of God best works

His work in the heart. Rather, a strong consciousness of His presence, and a clear communion with the Father and the Son, will do more in an hour than His absence for an age. Joy in the Holy Spirit will far more effectively purify the soul than the lack of that joy. And the peace of God is the best means of refining the soul from the refuse of earthly affections. Remove the false belief that the kingdom of God is divided against itself, so that the peace of God and joy in the Holy Spirit are obstacles to righteousness. We are saved by faith, not by unbelief, and blessed by hope, never by despair.

As long as men imagine such things, they may well walk in darkness. That effect will not end until the cause is removed. Yet we must not imagine darkness will immediately cease, even when the cause is no more. When either ignorance or sin has caused darkness, and that cause is removed, the light that was obstructed may not immediately return. That, too, is a free gift of God. He may restore it, sooner or later, according to His will. In the case of sin, we cannot reasonably expect the light to immediately return. Because the sin began before the punishment, it may justly remain after the sin is at an end. Even in the natural course of things, though a wound cannot be healed while an arrow is sticking in the flesh, neither is it healed as soon as the arrow is withdrawn. Soreness and pain may remain long after.

Finally, if darkness is caused by many heavy and unexpected temptations, the best way of removing and preventing this is to teach believers always to expect temptation. We live in an evil world, among wicked, subtle, malicious spirits, and have hearts capable of all evil. Teach that the whole work of perfection is not, as they imagined, done at once. When we first believe, we are as newborn babes who gradually grow up. We may expect many spiritual storms before coming to the full image of Jesus. Above all, let everyone be instructed, when the storm is upon them, not to reason with the devil, but to pray. Then pour out your soul before God and show Him your trouble.

To all persons in temptation and darkness, apply the great and precious promises, but don't apply them to the ignorant until their ignorance is removed, much less to an unrepentant sinner. To all these, largely and affectionately declare the lovingkindness of God our Savior, teaching and expounding on His tender mercies. Dwell upon the faithfulness of God, whose Word is tried to the uttermost, and on the virtue of that blood shed for us to cleanse us from all sin. God will then bear witness to His Word, and bring souls out of darkness and trouble. God will say, "Arise, shine, for your light has come, and my glory is risen upon you." That light, if you walk humbly and closely with God, will shine more and more unto the perfect day.

9

Heaviness Through Manifold Temptations

Now for a season, if need be, ye are in heaviness through manifold temptations. (1 Peter 1:6)

In the preceding chapter, I looked at that darkness of mind into which many who once walked in God's light have often fallen. Closely related to this is the heaviness of soul, which is even more common among believers. Indeed, almost all Christians experience this in some degree. So great is the resemblance between darkness and heaviness that they are frequently confused. We are apt to say, indifferently, here is one in darkness, or there is one in heaviness, as if they were equivalent terms, implying one is no different than the other.

But they are far different. Darkness is one thing; heaviness is another. There is a difference, a wide and essential difference, between the former and the latter. Unless Christians carefully note the difference, nothing will be more easy than for them to slide out of heaviness into darkness. In order to prevent this, I will attempt to show who these persons were, to whom Peter says, "Ye are in heaviness." I will fur-

Taken from John Wesley's, *Sermons on Several Occasions*, "Heaviness Through Manifold Temptations," XLVII, Vol. 1, p. 417 ff.

ther attempt to explain what kind of heaviness they were in, what were the causes of it, and what were the ends of it, concluding with some inferences.

Let us review what manner of persons these were who were in heaviness. There is no dispute they were believers at the time Peter addressed them. He expressly says this in verse 5, "[You] who are kept by the power of God through faith unto salvation." Again, in verse 7, he mentions the trial of their faith, much more precious than that of gold, which perishes. Yet again, in verse 9, he speaks of their receiving the end of their faith, the salvation of their souls. Therefore, at the same time they were in heaviness, they still possessed living faith. Their heaviness did not destroy their faith. They still endured in this faith.

Neither did their heaviness destroy their peace, the peace that passes all understanding, which is an inseparable part of true living faith. This we may easily gather from the second verse, in which Peter prays, not that grace and peace may be given them, but only that it may be multiplied to them, that the blessing that they already enjoyed might be more abundantly bestowed upon them.

The persons to whom Peter speaks here were also full of a living hope, for in verse 3, he says, "Blessed be the God and Father of our Lord Jesus Christ, which according to his abundant mercy hath begotten us again." This is you and I—all of us who are sanctified by the Spirit, and enjoy the sprinkling of the blood of Jesus Christ, along with a living hope of an inheritance, incorruptible, undefiled, and that does not fade away. So, regardless of their heaviness, they continued in hope of full immortality.

They still rejoiced in hope of the glory of God. They were filled with joy in the Holy Spirit. So, in verse 8, Peter having just mentioned the final revelation of Jesus Christ, namely, when He comes to judge the world, immediately adds, "In whom, though now ye see him not [not with your bodily eyes], yet believing, ye rejoice with joy unspeakable and full of glory." Their heaviness, therefore, was not only consistent with living hope but also with joy unspeakable. At the same time that they were heavy, they nevertheless rejoiced with joy full of glory.

In the midst of their heaviness, they also still enjoyed the love of God, which had been shed abroad in their hearts. Peter said, "Whom, having not seen, ye love." Though you have not yet seen Him face to face, yet knowing Him by faith, you have obeyed His word, "My son, give me thy heart." He is your God, and your love, the desire of your eyes, and your exceeding great reward. You have sought and found happiness in Him. You delight in the Lord, and He has given you your heart's desire.

Again, though they were heavy, still they were holy. They retained the same power over sin. They were still kept from this by the power of God. They were obedient children, not fashioned according to their former desires, but as He that had called them is holy, so were they holy in all things. Knowing they were redeemed by the precious blood of Jesus, as a lamb without spot and without blemish, they, through the faith and hope they had in God, had purified their souls by the Spirit. Upon the whole, their heaviness dwelt well with faith, with hope, with love of God and man, with the peace of God, with joy in the Holy Spirit, and with inward and outward holiness. It in no way impaired, much less destroyed, any part of the work of God in their hearts. It did not at all interfere with that sanctification of the Spirit that is at the root of all true obedience, nor with the happiness that results from grace and peace reigning in the heart.

We may easily learn what kind of heaviness they were in, which is the second thing to be seen. The word in the original Greek means "made sorry, grieved." This is the constant, literal meaning of the word. There is no ambiguity in the expression, nor any difficulty in understanding it. The persons spoken of here were grieved. The heaviness they were in was neither more nor less than sorrow or grief, a passion every child of man is well acquainted with.

It is probable English translators rendered the word as

"heaviness," to denote two things. First, the degree, and next, the continuance of it. It does seem this is a great degree of grief, a grief that makes a strong impression upon, and sinks deep into, the soul. Neither does this appear to be a transient sorrow, such as passes away in an hour. Rather, having taken fast hold of the heart, it is not soon shaken off. It continues for some time as a settled temper rather than a passion, even in those who have a living faith in Christ and the genuine love of God in their hearts.

Even in these, this heaviness may sometimes be so deep as to overshadow the whole soul and color all the affections, affecting the whole behavior. It may likewise have an influence over the body, particularly in those who are either of a naturally weak constitution or weakened by some accidental disorder, especially of the nervous kind. In many cases, we find the corruptible body presses down the soul. In this, the soul presses down the body and weakens it more and more. A deep and lasting sorrow of heart may sometimes weaken even a strong constitution, laying the foundation of bodily disorders that cannot be easily removed. Yet all this may exist along with a measure of that faith which still works by love.

This may well be termed a fiery trial, and though it is not the same as the one Peter speaks of in the fourth chapter, yet many of the expressions used there concerning outward sufferings may be applied to this inward affliction. They cannot, with any propriety, be applied to those who are in darkness, the ones who do not, and cannot, rejoice. Neither is it true of those in darkness that the Spirit of God and His glory rests upon them. But He frequently stays near those who are in heaviness, so that, though sorrowful, yet they are always rejoicing.

The Causes of Heaviness

Peter clearly states, you are in heaviness through manifold temptations. "Manifold," not only many in number, but of many kinds, varied and diversified a thousand ways by the change or addition of countless circumstances. This diversity and variety make it more difficult to guard against them.

Among these, we may include all bodily disorders, particularly acute diseases and violent pain of every kind, whether affecting the whole body or the smallest part of it. Some who have enjoyed uninterrupted health, experiencing none of this, may make light of them and doubt that sickness or bodily pain should bring heaviness upon the mind. Perhaps one in a thousand is of so strong a constitution as not to feel pain like most others. For whatever reasons, it has pleased God to show His almighty power by producing some of these prodigies of nature. They seem not to feel pain at all, even of the severest kind.

It is, in general, a fair observation that "pain is perfect misery, and in extreme—quite overturns all patience." Even where this is prevented by the grace of God, where men do possess their souls in patience, nevertheless, pain may cause much inner heaviness by the soul sympathizing with the body.

Diseases of long duration, though some are less painful, are apt to produce the same effect. When God allows consumption, or the chilling and burning fever, if it is not speedily removed, it will not only consume the eyes but cause sorrow of the heart. This is the case with those termed "nervous disorders." Faith does not overturn the course of nature. Natural causes still produce natural effects. Faith no more hinders the sinking of the spirits, as it is called, in a hysterical illness than the raising of the pulse in a fever.

When calamity comes as a whirlwind, and poverty as an armed man, is this a little temptation? Is it strange if it brings sorrow and heaviness? Although this also may appear but a small thing to those who stand at a distance, or who look and pass by on the other side, yet it is significant to them who feel it. We may, if the love of God is in our hearts, be content with food and lodging. But what shall they do who have neither of these, and can only embrace the rocks for a shelter, lie on the earth, and have only the sky for cover? What shall they do who have not a dry, or warm, much less a clean abode for themselves and their little ones, and no clothing to keep themselves or those they love from distressing cold?

Toiling for food is a pronounced curse upon man, requiring us to earn it by the sweat of the brow. But how many are there in this Christian country who toil and labor and sweat, and still do not have it, and continue to struggle with weariness and hunger? Is it not worse for one, after a hard day's labor, to come back to a poor, cold, dirty, uncomfortable lodging, and find there not even the food that is necessary to repair his wasted strength?

You who live at ease in the earth, who lack nothing but eyes to see, ears to hear, and hearts to understand how well God has dealt with you, is it not worse to seek bread day by day and find none? Consider the pain of having five or six children crying for what you cannot give. Were it not that such a person is restrained by an unseen hand, would he not soon curse God and die? Oh, hunger, hunger! Who knows what this means until he has felt it himself? I am astonished hunger brings no more than heaviness even in those who believe.

Perhaps next to this we may place the death of those who were near and dear to us, be it a tender parent, still in the prime of life, a beloved child who is rising into life and clasping about our heart, or a friend who was like our own soul, next to the grace of God, the best gift of heaven. A thousand circumstances may enhance the distress. Perhaps the child, or the friend, died in our embrace, perhaps was snatched away when we were not expecting it, flourishing, yet cut down like a flower. In all these cases, we not only may but ought to be affected. It is the design of God that we should. He would not have us be like sticks and stones. He would have our affections regulated, not extinguished. Therefore, nature unreproved may drop a tear. There may be sorrow without sin.

We may feel a still deeper sorrow for those who are dead while they live on account of unkindness, ingratitude, or death of faith. Who can express what a lover of persons may feel for a friend, or a brother or sister, who is dead to God? For a husband, a wife, a parent, a child rushing into sin as a horse into battle, and, despite all arguments and persuasions, hastens to work out his own damnation? This anguish of spirit may be heightened to an inconceivable degree by the memory that he who is now racing to destruction once followed well in God's way of life. Whatever he was in time past serves now only to make our reflections on what he is more piercing and distressing.

In all these circumstances, we may be assured Satan will be waiting to improve his opportunity. He who is always walking about, seeking whom he may devour, will then, especially, use all his power, all his skill, to gain any advantage over the soul of one who is already cast down. Satan will never be sparing in his torments of those who are most likely to fall from assaults on their hearts. He will suggest that God does not care and does not govern the earth, or at least that He does not govern it correctly by the rules of justice and mercy. He will attempt to stir up the heart against God in order to renew our natural enmity against Him. And if we attempt to fight him with his own weapons, if we begin to reason with him, more and more heaviness will undoubtedly ensue, if not utter darkness.

It has been frequently supposed that there is still another cause, if not of darkness, at least of heaviness, namely God's withdrawing himself from the soul because it is His sovereign will to do so. Certainly He will do this if we grieve His Holy Spirit, either by outward or inward sin, either by doing evil or neglecting to do good, by giving way either to pride or anger, to spiritual sloth, to foolish desire, or inordinate affection. I absolutely deny that He ever withdraws himself merely because it is His good pleasure. There is no text in the Bible that gives any grounds for such an idea. It is a supposition contrary, not only to many particular texts, but to the whole meaning of Scripture. It is repugnant to the very nature of God. It is utterly beneath His majesty and wisdom "to play bo-peep with His creatures." It is inconsistent both with His justice and mercy, and with the sound experience of all His children.

One more cause of heaviness is mentioned by many of those who are termed mystic authors. This notion has crept in, I know not how, even among unlearned people who do not read the mystics. I cannot explain this better than in the words of a lady who relates her personal experience. "I continued so happy in my beloved Jesus, that, although I should have been forced to live as a vagabond in a desert, I should have found no difficulty in it. This state had not lasted long, when, in effect, I found myself led into a desert. I found myself in a forlorn condition, altogether poor, wretched, and miserable. The proper source of this grief is the knowledge of ourselves, by which we find that there is an extreme difference between God and us. We see ourselves most opposite to Him, and that our inmost soul is entirely corrupted, depraved, and full of all kinds of evil and malignity, of the world and the flesh, and all sorts of abominations." From this it has been inferred that the knowledge of ourselves, without which we should perish everlastingly, must, even after we have attained justifying faith, cause the deepest heaviness.

But upon this I would observe, in the preceding paragraph, this person also says, "Hearing I had not a true faith in Christ, I offered myself up to God, and immediately felt His love." It may be so, and yet it does not appear that this was justification. It is more probable it was no more than what are usually termed the drawings of the Father. If so, the heaviness and darkness that followed her original experience was nothing more than conviction of sin, which, in the nature of things, must precede that faith by which we are justified. Suppose she was justified immediately; there was then no time for that gradual increasing self-knowledge which precedes justification. In this case, therefore, it came after, and was probably the more severe because it was not expected.

There is a far deeper, a far clearer and fuller knowledge of our inbred sin, of our total corruption by nature, after justification, than there ever was before it. But this need not cause darkness of soul. I will not say that it must bring us into heaviness. If that were so, Peter would not have said "if need be," for there would be an absolute, indispensable need of it for all who would know the perfect love of God and thereby be made able to be partakers of the inheritance of the saints of light. But this is by no means the case. On the contrary, God may increase the knowledge of ourselves to any degree, and increase, in the same proportion, the knowledge of himself and the experience of His love. In this case there would be no desert, no misery, no forlorn condition, but love, and peace, and joy, gradually springing up into everlasting life.

Heaviness: God's Purifying Agent

For what purpose, then, does God permit heaviness to befall so many of His children? Peter gives us a plain and direct answer to this important question in verse 7. "That the trial of your faith, being more precious than of gold that perisheth, though it be tried with fire, might be found unto praise and honour, and glory at the appearing of Jesus Christ." There may be an allusion to this, in that well-known passage of the fourth chapter, although it primarily relates to quite another thing, as has already been observed. "Think it not strange concerning the fiery trial which is to try you. . . . But rejoice, inasmuch as ye are partakers of Christ's sufferings; that, when his glory shall be revealed, ye may be glad also with exceeding joy" (1 Pet. 4:12,13).

We learn, then, the first and main purpose of God's permitting the temptations that bring heaviness on His children. It is the trial of their faith, which is tried by these, even as gold by the fire. Now we know gold tried in the fire is purified, separated from its dross. So is faith in the fire of temptation. The more it is tried, the more it is purified. Not only is it purified, but strengthened, confirmed, increased abundantly, by so many more proofs of the wisdom and power, the love and faithfulness of God.

This, then, to increase our faith, is one gracious end of God's permitting these manifold temptations. They serve to try, to purify, to confirm, and increase that living hope also to which end the God and Father of our Lord Jesus Christ has begotten us again of His abundant mercy.

Our hope cannot but increase in the same proportion as our faith. On this foundation it stands. Believing in His name, living by faith in the Son of God, we hope for, we have a confident expectation of, the glory which shall be revealed. Consequently, whatever strengthens our faith also increases our hope. At the same time it increases our joy in the Lord, which can only attend a hope full of immortality. In this view, Peter exhorts believers to "rejoice, inasmuch as ye are partakers of Christ's sufferings," adding, "Happy are ye; for the spirit of glory and of God resteth upon you." You are hereby enabled, even in the midst of sufferings, to rejoice with joy unspeakable and full of glory. They rejoice more, because the trials that increase their faith and hope also increase their love—both their gratitude to God for all His mercies and their goodwill to all mankind. Accordingly, the more aware they are of the lovingkindness of God their Savior, the more their heart is inflamed with love to Him who first loved us. The clearer and stronger evidence they have of the glory that shall be revealed, the more they love Him who has purchased it for them and given them the assurance of it. This, the increase of their love, is another end of the temptations permitted to come upon them.

Yet another is their advance in holiness—holiness of the heart, and holiness of conduct, the latter naturally resulting from the former, for a good tree will bring forth good fruit. All inward holiness is the immediate fruit of the faith that works by love. By this the Spirit purifies the heart from pride, self-will, passion, from love of the world, from foolish and harmful desires, from vile and vain affections. Besides that, sanctified afflictions have, through the grace of God, an immediate and direct tendency to holiness. Through the operation of His Spirit, they humble more and more, and abase the soul before God. They calm and subdue our turbulent spirit, tame the fierceness of our nature, soften our obstinacy and self-will, crucify us to the world, and bring us to expect all our strength from, and to seek all our happiness in, God.

All these terminate in that great purpose: that our faith, hope, love, and holiness may be found, if they do not yet appear, unto praise, from God himself, and honor, from men and angels, and glory, assigned by the great Judge, to all who have endured to the end. This will be assigned in that final day to every man according to his works, according to the work that God has done in his heart, and the outward works he has done for God. It is also done according to what he has suffered, so that all these trials bring unspeakable gain. In so many ways, these light afflictions, which are but for a moment, work out for us a far more exceeding and eternal weight of glory.

Add to this the advantage that others may receive by seeing our behavior under affliction; example frequently makes a deeper impression on people than words. What example has stronger influence, not only on those who are partakers of the same precious faith, but even on them who have not known God, than that of a soul calm and serene in the midst of storms—a soul sorrowful, yet always rejoicing, meekly accepting whatever is the will of God, however grievous it may be to nature. A soul saying, in sickness and pain, "The cup which my Father hath given me, shall I not drink it?" (John 18:11) and in loss or need, "The Lord gave, and the Lord hath taken away; blessed be the name of the Lord" (Job 1:21).

Let us conclude and note some inferences. First, wide is the difference between darkness of soul and heaviness, which are so generally confused with each other, even by experienced Christians. Darkness, or the wilderness state, implies a total loss of joy in the Holy Spirit. Heaviness does not. In the midst of this we may rejoice with joy unspeakable. Those who are in darkness have lost the peace of God. Those who are in heaviness have not lost His peace; peace as well as grace may be multiplied unto them. In the former, the love of God has grown cold, if it is not utterly extinguished. In the latter, it retains its full force, or, rather, increases daily. In darkness, faith itself, if not totally lost, is greviously decayed. Their evidence and conviction of things not seen, particularly the pardoning love of God, is not so clear or strong as in time past, and their trust in Him is proportionately weakened. Those in heaviness, though they do not see Him, still have a clear, unshaken confidence in God, with an abiding evidence of His love by which all their sins are blotted out. As long as we can distinguish faith from unbelief, hope from despair, peace from war, the love of God from the love of the world, we may infallibly distinguish heaviness from darkness.

We learn from this that there may be need of heaviness, but there can be no need of darkness. There may be need of our being in heaviness for a season in order to accomplish the ends stated above—at least as a natural result of those manifold temptations that are necessary to try and to increase our faith, to confirm and enlarge our hope, to purify our heart from all unholy tempers, and to perfect us in love. By consequence, they are necessary to brighten our crown and add to our eternal weight of glory. But we cannot say that darkness is necessary in order to achieve any of those results. It is in no way conducive to them. The loss of faith, hope, and love is surely neither conducive to holiness nor to the increase of that reward in heaven that will be in proportion to our holiness on earth.

From Peter's manner of speaking, we may gather that even heaviness is not always necessary. "Now for a season, if need be," means it is not necessary for all persons, nor for any person at all times. God is able; He has both power and wisdom to work, when He pleases, the same work of grace in any soul by other means. In some instances, He does so.

He causes those, whom it pleases Him, to go on from strength to strength until they perfect holiness with almost no heaviness at all. Having an absolute power over the heart of man, He can move all the springs of it at His pleasure. But these cases are rare. God generally sees it as good to try acceptable men in the furnace of affliction so that manifold temptations and heaviness, more or less, are usually the portion of His dearest children.

We ought, therefore, to watch and pray, and use our strongest attempts to avoid falling into darkness. But we need not try to avoid, as much as try to improve, heaviness. Our greatest concern is to behave ourselves under it, and to wait upon the Lord in it, so it may fully answer all the plan of His love that permitted it to come upon us. It is His means of increasing our faith, of confirming our hope, of perfecting us in all holiness. When heaviness comes, remember these gracious ends for which it is permitted, and use all diligence to avoid making void the counsel of God against ourselves. Earnestly work together with Him, with the grace that He is continually giving us, to purify ourselves from all pollution, both of flesh and spirit, and daily grow in the grace of our Lord Jesus Christ until we are received into His everlasting kingdom!

10

Friendship With the World

Ye adulterers and adulteresses, know ye not that the friendship of the world is enmity with God? whosoever therefore will be a friend of the world is the enemy of God. (James 4:4)

There is a passage in Paul's letter to the Romans that many have thought has the same meaning: "Be not conformed to this world" (Rom. 12:2). But these two are quite different. "Be not conformed" speaks of another thing. The imagined resemblance of the two arises merely from the use of the word *world* in both. This naturally leads us to think that Paul means "conformity to the world" to be the same as James's "friendship with the world." However, they are entirely different, as the words in the original Greek prove.

Paul's words contain an important direction to Christians. It is as if he had said, be not conformed to either the wisdom or the spirit, or the fashions of the age, of either the unconverted Jews, or heathens, among whom you live. You are called to show, by your whole life and behavior, that you are renewed in the Spirit in your mind, conforming to the image of the Creator. Show that your example is not the will

---

Taken from John Wesley's, *Sermons on Several Occasions*, "Friendship With the World," LXXXV, Vol. 2, p. 196 ff.

of man, but from the good, and acceptable, and perfect will of God.

It is not strange that James's caution against friendship with the world should be so misunderstood, even among Christians. I have not been able to find any author, ancient or modern, who has written on the subject at all. I have never heard one sermon preached on it, either before seminary or afterward. I never was in any group where it was discussed, even for an hour.

Yet there are very few subjects more important, few that so concern the very essence of Christianity—the life of God in the soul—and the continuance and increase, or the decay, even extinction of it. From lack of instruction on this subject, the most disastrous consequences have followed. These consequences have not affected those who were still dead in trespasses and sins, but they have fallen upon many of those who had become truly alive to God. They have affected many of those called "spirit-filled," in particular, perhaps more than any other people. I hope it is for lack of understanding this advice from James, rather than from any contempt for it, that many of these are sick, spiritually sick, and many others are asleep who were once thoroughly awake.

Many who were once greatly alive to God, and whose desires were in heaven, though they walked in all the commandments of God, though they still abounded in good works and abstained from all known sin, even from the appearance of evil, gradually and unknowingly fell away. They were like Jonah's gourd when the worm ate the root of it, so much so that they are less alive to God now than they were ten, twenty, or thirty years ago. But this is easily accounted for if we observe that as they increased in goods, they increased in friendship with the world, which, indeed, is always the case unless the mighty grace of God intervenes. In the same proportion as they increased in worldly gain, the life of God in their soul decreased.

This is not strange if these words are really the words of God: "Ye adulterers and adulteresses, know ye not that the friendship of the world is enmity with God?" Let us thoughtfully consider the meaning of this. May God open the eyes of our understanding, so that, in spite of all the mist in which the wisdom of the world would cover us, we may discern what is the good and acceptable will of God.

What Is "Friendship With the World"?

Let us first consider what James means here by the world. He does not refer to the outward frame of things called heaven and earth in Scripture, but to the inhabitants of earth, humans, or at least, the greater part of them. But which people? This is fully determined both by Jesus himself and by John, His beloved disciple. First, Jesus said, "If the world hate you, ye know that it hated me before it hated you. If ye were of the world, the world would love his own: but because ye are not of the world, but I have chosen you out of the world, therefore the world hateth you. . . . If they have persecuted me, they will also persecute you. . . . All these things will they do unto you for my name's sake because they know not him that sent me" (John 15:18–21).

You see here, the world is placed on one side, and those who are not of the world, on the other. Those whom God has chosen out of the world, sanctified by the Spirit to believe the truth, are set in direct opposition to those whom He has not so chosen. Yet again, these who "know not him that sent me," who know not God, they are the world.

Equally expressive are the words of John, "Marvel not, my brethren, if the world hate you. We know that we have passed from death unto life, because we love the brethren" (1 John 3:13), as if he had said, you must not expect that any should love you, except those who have also passed from death unto life. It follows, then, that those who are not passed from death unto life, who are not alive to God, are the world. We may learn the same thing in the words, "We know that we are of God, and the whole world lieth in wickedness" (1 John 5:19). Here "the world" plainly means those who are not of God, and who, consequently, belong to Satan.

On the contrary, those of God love God, or at least fear Him and keep His commandments. This is the first requirement of those who are of God. They are servants who have departed from evil and try to do good, walking in all His ways because they have the fear of God in their heart along with a sincere desire to please Him. Fix in your mind this plain meaning of the term "the world" as those who do not fear God. Let no man deceive you with words. It means no more and no less than this.

Understanding the term in this sense, what kind of friendship may we have with the world? We may, we ought, to love them as ourselves, for they are also included in the word neighbor. Bear them goodwill, and desire their happiness as sincerely as we desire the happiness of our own souls.

We are, in a sense, to honor them, as we are directed by the Bible to honor all men as the creatures of God, even as immortal spirits who are capable of knowing, of loving, and of enjoying Him to all eternity. We are to honor them as redeemable by the blood of Jesus, who tasted death for every man. We are to have compassion for them when we see them forsaking their own mercies, wandering from the path of life and rushing to everlasting destruction. We are never willingly to grieve their spirits, or give them any pain, but are to give them all the pleasure we innocently can, since we are to please all men for their good. We are never to aggravate their faults, but willingly to allow all the good that is in them.

We may speak to them as required, in the most gentle manner possible. We should speak no evil of them when they are absent unless it is absolutely necessary, unless it is the only means we know of preventing their doing wrong. Otherwise, we are to speak of them with all the respect we can without transgressing the bounds of truth. We are to behave toward them with courtesy, showing them all the regard we can without agreeing with their sins. We should do them all the good that is in our power, all they are willing to receive from us, following the universal example of our Father who is in heaven. God, until they will condescend to receive greater blessings, gives them as much grace as they are willing to accept. He causes the sun to rise on the evil and the good, and sends His rain on the just and on the unjust.

Does this mean, then, that we should have no relationship with ungodly men at all? Should we wholly avoid them? By no means. The opposite has been shown already. If we were not to have fellowship with them at all, we must go out of the world. Then we could not show them those kindnesses that we have already listed. We may relate to them on business when courtesy demands it. However, we must take great care not to carry it too far, and do so only when we have a reasonable hope of doing them good. Here, too, we have a special need of caution and much prayer, otherwise we may easily burn ourselves while striving to pluck other brands out of the fire.

We may easily hurt our own souls by sliding into a close attachment with any who do not know God. This is the friendship that is prohibited. We must be careful not to fall into this deadly snare, lest before we are aware, we contract a love or delight in them. We should have no needless relationship with them. It is our duty and wisdom to be with them no more often and no longer than is strictly necessary. During the whole time, we need to remember and follow the example of him who said in a psalm, "I will keep my mouth with a bridle, while the wicked is before me" (Ps. 39:1).

Look at the consequence when Jehoshaphat forgot this command and formed a relationship with Ahab. He first lost his substance. The ships they sent out were wrecked at Ezion-geber. When he was not content with this warning, as well as that of the prophet Micaiah, and went up with him to Ramoth-gilead, he was on the point of losing his life. We tread on sure ground only when we can say from the psalm, "To the saints that are in the earth, and to the excellent, in whom is all my delight" (Ps. 16:3).

Above all, we should tremble at the very thought of entering into a marriage covenant, the closest attachment of all, with any person who does not love, or at least fear, God. This is the greatest folly into which a child of God could possibly plunge. Marriage implies every sort of connection with the ungodly that a Christian, in conscience, is to avoid. No wonder, then, it is so flatly forbidden by God through Paul's expression, "Be ye not unequally yoked together with unbelievers" (2 Cor. 6:14). Nothing can be more clear, especially if we understand the unbeliever is one who is unable to say, "The life which I now live in the flesh I live by the faith of the Son of God, who loved me, and gave himself for me" (Gal. 2:20). Such a person has not even the faith of a servant. He does not fear God and work righteousness.

The Folly of Friendship With the World

The friendship of the world is absolutely prohibited and we are strictly required to abstain from it for two general reasons: first, because it is sin in itself; and second, because it is accompanied by dreadful consequences.

First, it is a sin in itself, and not a common sin, according to the Word of God. Friendship with the world is no less than spiritual adultery. All who are guilty of it are adulterers and adulteresses by the Holy Spirit. It is plainly a violation of our marriage contract with God. Loving the creature more than the Creator is flat contradiction to His command, "My son, give me thine heart" (Prov. 23:26).

It is a sin of the most abominable nature, not only implying ignorance of God and forgetfulness of Him, or inattention to Him, but positive enmity against God. It is openly, palpably so. James asks us, Can you possibly be ignorant of this plain truth, that friendship with the world is enmity against God? How terrible an inference he draws from this: whoever will be a friend of the world, of the men who do not know God, is constituted an enemy of God. Just the desire, whether successful or not, earns him that name, enemy of God.

As it is a sin, a very grievous sin in itself, so it has the most dreadful consequences. It frequently reentangles people in the commission of those sins from which they had once escaped. It generally makes them sharers of others' sins, even those they do not commit themselves. It gradually lessens their hatred and dread of sin in general, and thereby prepares them for falling easy prey to any strong temptation.

It also lays them open to all those sins of omission in which their worldly friends are guilty. It lessens their concern for private prayer, family duty, fasting, attending public worship, and partaking of holy communion. The indifference of those who are close to them, with respect to all these spiritual matters, will gradually influence them. Even if they do not say one word to recommend their own way, their example speaks and is many times more forceful than any words. By their worldly example, they are unavoidably betrayed almost continually into unprofitable and uncharitable conversation, till they no longer control their mouth and keep from speaking unspiritually. They can join in backbiting, tale bearing, and evil speaking without any check of conscience. Thus having so frequently grieved the Holy Spirit of God, He no longer reproves them for it. Their speech is no longer seasoned with salt and able to minister grace.

But these are not all the deadly consequences that result from association with unholy people. It not only hinders them from godly conversation, but directly tends to corrupt the heart. It tends to create or increase in us all that pride and self-sufficiency, all that resentfulness, and every irregular passion and wrong disposition in which their companions indulge. It gently leads them into habitual self-indulgence and unwillingness to deny themselves. With that comes unreadiness to bear or take up any cross, a softness and delicacy, and the fear of others that brings numberless snares. It draws Christians back into the love of the world, into foolish and harmful desires, into the desire of the flesh, the desire of the eyes, and the pride of life, until they are swallowed up in them. The result is, in the end, the last state of such Christians is far worse than the first.

If Christians will connect themselves with those of the world, even if the latter should not try to make them like themselves, they will actually accomplish it. I do not know how to account for the fact that their worldly spirit is infectious. While you are near them, you are apt to catch their spirit, whether they will it or not. Physicians have warned that almost every disease of man is more or less infectious. Likewise, so are spiritual diseases.

Spiritual infection is not so swiftly communicated by some as it is by others. In either case, the person already diseased does not desire or plan to infect another. The man who has the plague does not desire or intend to communicate his illness to you. But this does not make you safe, so keep your distance, or you will surely be infected.

Experience shows that the same is true of diseases of the mind. Suppose the proud, the vain, the passionate, the wanton do not desire or plan to infect you with their own distempers, yet it is best to keep at a distance from them. You are not safe if you come too near them. You will perceive, hopefully not too late, that their very breath is infectious.

It has been discovered that there is a spiritual atmosphere surrounding every human body, which naturally affects everyone who comes within the limits of it. If you continue long within another's worldly atmosphere, you can hardly escape being infected. The contagion spreads from soul to soul, even if the persons do not intend or desire it. And beyond that, it is a notorious truth that many men of the world eagerly desire to make their companions like themselves, and even use every means, with their utmost skill and energy, to accomplish their desire. Therefore, flee for your life. Do not play with the fire, but escape before flames ignite upon you. But how many pleas there are for friendship with the world. How strong are the temptations to it. Let us consider some of the most dangerous, and at the same time most common.

We begin with one that is the most dangerous, and very common. "I grant," says one, "the person I am about to marry is not a religious person. She does not pretend or claim to be, and has thought little about it. But she is a beautiful creature, extremely agreeable, and I think she will make a lovely companion."

This is one of the greatest snares tempting human nature. This is a temptation that no power of man is able to overcome. Nothing less than the mighty power of God can make a way for you to escape from it. He can work a complete deliverance. His grace is sufficient for you, but only if you work with Him, only if you deny yourself and take up your cross. What you do, you must do at once, and not by degrees. You must immediately cut off the relationship and cast it from you. There is no time for conferring with others. Immediately, conquer or perish.

Let us turn the tables. Suppose a woman who loves God is courted by an agreeable man, genteel, lively, entertaining, suitable in all other respects, but not a Christian. What should she do in such a case? What she should do, if she believes the Bible, is quite clear. She should hold fast to the shield of faith and earnestly cry to the Lord for strength, for none but one who gives herself to watching and prayer, and perseveres in them, can overcome. If she does this, she will be a happy Christian witness in the midst of an unbelieving world. Since all things are possible with God, so all things are possible to her who believes.

But either a man or a woman may ask, "What if the person seeking his fellowship is a well-educated person of strong natural understanding?" Fellowship with such a person can be a learning experience, "improving the understanding," it is claimed. It may improve the understanding, and knowledge may be imparted, but the loss will be greater than the gain if the person has not the least concern about God. In such a case, you can hardly avoid decreasing in holiness as much as you increase in knowledge. If you lose one degree of inward or outward holiness, all the knowledge you gain will not be adequate compensation.

If the proposed partner's fine understanding is not his

main quality, yet he has many other valuable qualifications, such as good humor, compassion, and generosity, then he is even infinitely more dangerous if he does not regard God. If you have any close relationship with a person of this character, you will surely absorb his spirit. It is hardly possible for you to avoid stopping just where he stops. I have found nothing so difficult in all my life as to associate with men of this kind—good sort of men—as they are commonly called, without being hurt by them. Beware of them and have only as much to do with them as business requires, or as God leads in witnessing to them. Otherwise, though you do not feel any present harm, yet by slow and imperceptible degrees, they will turn you again to earthly things and quench the life of God in your soul.

It may be that persons who seek your fellowship are not experienced in Christianity, but understand it, so that you reap some new knowledge from their conversation. If this is really the case, it seems you may associate with them as teachers, but very sparingly and cautiously, or you will lose more of your spiritual life than all the knowledge you gain is worth.

Then comes this objection, "But the persons in question are useful to me in carrying on my worldly business. On many occasions they are so necessary to me that I could not carry it on well without them."

Instances of this kind frequently occur. This is a sufficient reason for having some relationship, perhaps frequently, with men who do not fear God. But even this is no reason for entering into intimate friendship with those persons. Here you need to be most careful, lest even by necessary dealings to increase your fortune in the world, the grace of God should decrease in your soul.

There may be one more plausible reason given for some intimacy with an unholy man. You may say, "I have been helpful to him. I have assisted him when he was in trouble, and he remembers it with gratitude. He esteems and loves me, though he does not love God. Should I not then care for him and return love for love? Do not even heathens do so?" I answer, you should certainly return love for love, but it does not follow that you should have any intimacy with him. That would be at the peril of your soul. Let your love express itself in constant and fervent prayer. Pray to God for him, but do not let your love for him carry you so far as to weaken, if not destroy, your own soul.

"But must I not be intimate with my family, whether they fear God or not? Has not His providence given them to me?" Yes, it has, but there are close and distant relations. The closest relations are husbands and wives. Because these have taken each other for better or worse, they must make the best of each other. God has joined them together, and none should put them apart, unless in the case of adultery, or when the life of one or the other is in imminent danger. Parents are almost nearly as close with their children. You cannot part with them while they are young. It is your duty to train them up with all care in the way in which they should go. How frequently you should be in their company when they are grown up can be determined by Christian prudence. This also will determine how long it is expedient for children, if it is their own choice, to remain with their parents. In general, if your children do not fear God, you should leave them as soon as is convenient. But even then, take care, if it is in your power, that they do not lack the necessities or conveniences of life. As for other relations, even brothers or sisters, if they are of the world, you are under no obligation to be in fellowship with them. You may be civil and friendly at a distance.

Since friendship of the world is enmity against God, and the best and only way to heaven is to avoid all intimacy with worldly men, how can one resolve to avoid such intimacy? Who, even among those who love or fear God can do it? I have known a few, who, even in this respect, were lights in a darkened land. They did not and would not either contract or continue any association even with persons of the most refined and improved understanding and the most engaging dispositions, merely because they were of the world and not concerned with God. Although the worldly persons were capable of assisting them in business, or of improving their knowledge, these few shunned the worldly ones, even when they were admired and esteemed for that very religion which they themselves had not experienced. The steadfast Christian resolutely refrained from all familiarity even with these, for the sake of conscience.

"Go thou and do likewise," whoever you are, who are a child of God by faith. At whatever cost, flee spiritual adultery, and have no friendship with the world. However tempted by profit or pleasure, contract no intimacy with worldly-minded men. If you have contracted any such already, break it off without delay. If your ungodly friend is as dear to you as your right eye, or as useful as your right hand, still, waste no time, but "pluck out the right eye," or "cut off the right hand," and cast them from you. It is not an indifferent thing. Your life is at stake—eternal life or eternal death. Is it not better to go into life having one eye or one hand than having both cast into hellfire? When you knew no better, God winked at the times of ignorance. But now your eyes are opened, now the light has come, walk in the light! Do not touch tar, lest you be soiled. At all events, keep yourself pure.

Whatever others do, whether they will hear or whether they will forbear, hear this, all you who are called Christians. However pressed or tempted to do so, have no friendship with the world. Look around and see the sad effects it has produced among your brothers and sisters. How many of the mighty have fallen by this very thing because they refused all warning.

They would intimately associate with earthly-minded men until they "measured back their steps to earth again!" Oh, come out from among them, from all unholy men, however harmless they may appear, and be separate—at least as far as to have no intimacy with them. Your fellowship is to be with the Father and with His Son Jesus Christ. Let it be with those, and those only, who at least seek the Lord Jesus in sincerity. Then you shall be, in a peculiar sense, my sons and daughters, says the Lord Almighty.

11

In What Sense We Are to Leave the World

Come out from among them, and be ye separate, saith the Lord, and touch not the unclean thing; and I will receive you, And will be a Father unto you, and ye shall be my sons and daughters, saith the Lord Almighty. (2 Corinthians 6:17, 18)

Few Christians have ever meditated on this scripture. We have read this, but have never taken it to heart, or seen that it contains as plain and explicit a commandment as any in the whole Bible. There are still fewer who understand the true meaning of this instruction.

Many have interpreted this verse as a command to come out of the established church. A great number of sermons have been preached, books written, and many pious men have based their separation from the church chiefly on this text. "God himself," they say, "commands us, 'Come out from among them, and be ye separate.' And it is only on this condition that He will receive us, and we shall be the sons and daughters of the Lord Almighty."

But this interpretation is totally foreign to the mind of

Taken from John Wesley's, *Sermons on Several Occasions*, "In What Sense We Are to Leave the World," LXXXVI, Vol. 2, p. 204 ff.

Paul, who is not speaking here of any church but on another subject. Neither Paul nor any of his brethren draw such inference from the words. If they had done so, it would have been in flat contradiction both to the example and teachings of Jesus. Although the Jewish congregation was then as unclean and unholy as any Christian church now on earth, our Lord continued attending those services. He directed His followers in this, as in every other respect, to follow His way. That is clearly implied in the remarkable passage, "The scribes and the Pharisees sit in Moses' seat: all therefore whatsoever they bid you observe, that observe and do; but do not ye after their works: for they say and do not" (Matthew 23:2–3). Even though the Scribes and Pharisees themselves say but do not, though their lives contradict their doctrines, though they are ungodly men, yet Jesus here permits, and requires, His disciples to hear them. He requires them to observe and do what they say. The disciples could not do that unless they heard them.

Accordingly, the apostles, as long as they were at Jerusalem, constantly attended the public service. Certainly these words do not call for a separation from the established church. Neither do they refer to the direction Paul gives in his first letter to the Corinthians. That whole passage runs:

> I wrote unto you in an epistle not to company with fornicators: Yet not altogether with the fornicators of this world, or with the covetous, or extortioners, or with idolaters; for then must ye needs go out of the world. But now I have written unto you not to keep company, if any man that is called a brother be a fornicator, or covetous, or an idolater, or a railer, or a drunkard, or an extortioner; with such an one, no not to eat. (1 Cor. 5:9–11)

This injunction pertains to those who are members of the same Christian community. Paul does not command them to stay away from heathens or from men in general. He adds the reason, "For then must ye needs go out of the world." You could transact no business in the world because it is filled with all these sins. But if any man called a brother, or connected with you as a Christian, is a fornicator, or covet-

ous, or an idolator, or a railer, or a drunkard, or an extortioner, don't break bread with him.

How important this caution is, but how little it is observed, even by those who seem to be conscientious Christians. Indeed, some parts of the command are not easily followed for a plain reason. They are not easy to understand. I
mean, it is not easy to understand to whom Paul refers. It is
very difficult, for instance, to know, except in some glaring
cases, who is an extortioner, or covetous. We can hardly know
one or the other without seeming to be busybodies in other
men's affairs. Yet the prohibition is as strong concerning
fellowship with these as with fornicators or adulterers. We
can only act in the simplicity of our hearts, without being
infallible judges, always willing to be better informed according to the best information available.

Although this direction relates only to our Christian
brothers and sisters, the text is far wider, and it doubtless
refers to all people. The admonition clearly requires us to
keep a distance from all ungodly men. The word we translate
"unclean thing," might better be rendered "unclean person,"
probably alluding to the ceremonial law, which forbade
touching one who was legally unclean.

Even here, if we were to understand the expression literally, taking the words in the strictest sense, the same absurdity would follow. We would have to, as Paul says, go out
of the world; we would not be able to remain in the profes-
sions in which God has placed us. If we were not to associate
at all with men such as these, it would be impossible to transact our daily business. Then every conscientious Christian
could only flee into the desert. It would not be enough to turn
into recluses and to shut ourselves up in monasteries or con-
vents, for even then we would have some relationship with
ungodly men in order to obtain the necessities of life. Paul's
words, therefore, must necessarily be understood with considerable reservation. They do not prohibit our fellowship
with any man, good or bad, in our worldly business.

Many occasions will occur in which we must deal with

them in order to transact those affairs that cannot be done otherwise. Some of these may require us to have association with drunkards or fornicators. It even may be necessary for us to spend a considerable amount of time in their company, otherwise we should not be able to fulfill the duties of our Christian calling. Therefore, such closeness with men holy or unholy is in no way contrary to Paul's advice.

Then what is it he forbids? It is intimacy with ungodly men when there is no reason or business that requires it, along with a friendship deeper than business requires. He forbids spending more time in their company than is necessary to finish our business. Also, he forbids choosing ungodly persons, however ingenious or agreeable, to be our ordinary companions or our familiar friends. If any example has less excuse than others, it is that which Paul expressly forbids elsewhere, being unequally yoked with an unbeliever in marriage.

I know of nothing that can justify this, not the senses, wit, or beauty of the person, nor any temporary advantage, nor fear of want, nor even the command of a parent. If any parent commands what is contrary to the Word of God, the child ought to obey God rather than the parent. This prohibition is laid down in the preceding verses: "What fellowship hath righteousness with unrighteousness? and what communion hath light with darkness? And what concord hath Christ with Belial? or what part hath he that believeth with an infidel?" (2 Cor. 6:14–15). You are the temple of the living God. God has said, "I will dwell in them, and walk in them; and I will be their God, and they shall be my people." It follows, "Wherefore come out from among them"—the unrighteous, the children of darkness, the sons of Belial, the unbelievers—"and be ye separate . . . and touch not the unclean thing," or person, "and I will receive you."

Purpose of the Prohibition

Here is the basis of the commandment not to have any more familiarity with unholy men than is absolutely necessary. There can be no more profitable fellowship between the righteous and the unrighteous than there can be communion between light and darkness, whether of natural or spiritual darkness. As Jesus can have no agreement with the devil, so a believer in Him can have no agreement with an unbeliever.

It is absurd to imagine that any true union could exist between two persons while one of them remains in spiritual darkness and the other walks in the light. They are subjects not only of two separate, but of two opposite, kingdoms. They act upon quite different principles; they aim at quite different ends. It necessarily follows that frequently these persons will walk in different paths. How can they walk together until they are in agreement, and both serve either Christ or Satan?

What are the consequences of our not obeying this directive to come out from among unholy men and be separate from them, not contracting or keeping a familiar relationship with them? Visible, harmful consequences probably will not immediately be apparent. Disobedience will hardly lead us immediately into any outward sin. It may not immediately cause neglect of an outward duty. However, it will first sap the foundations of Christianity, and little by little dampen our zeal for God. It will gently cool our fervency of spirit that accompanied our first love. Even if they do not openly oppose anything we say or do, by degrees their spirit will affect our spirit, transfusing into it their lukewarmness and indifference toward God and the things of God. It will weaken our soul, destroy the vigor of our spirit, and cause us to slacken our pace in running the race that is set before us.

By the same degree, needless association with unholy people will weaken our divine evidence and conviction of things unseen. It will dim the eyes of our soul by which we see Him who is invisible, weakening our confidence in Him. It will gradually abate our yearning for the world to come, and deaden the hope that allowed us to sit next to Christ

Jesus. It will imperceptibly cool the flame of love that caused us to cry, "Whom have I in heaven but thee? and there is none upon earth that I desire beside thee" (Psalm 73:25). Thus it strikes at the root of our vital Christianity, and of our fellowship with the Father and the Son.

By the same degree, and in the same secret and unobserved manner, it will prepare us to measure our steps back to earth again. It softly sinks us into the love of the world from which we had escaped, to fall gently into the desire of the flesh, seeking happiness in the pleasures of sense, the desires of the eye, the pleasures of imagination, and the pride of life, the seeking of it in pomp, in riches, or in the praise of man. All this is done by Satan before we are aware of his attack or are conscious of our loss.

But it is more than just the love of the world that steals in while we fraternize with those of a worldly spirit. Every other evil passion and temper of which the human soul is capable follows. In particular, pride, vanity, judgment, evil gossip, and the strong inclination to revenge come back. On the other hand, frivolity, gaiety, and dissipation infect us and increase continually. We know how these abound in all who do not know God. They will work their way into all who frequently and freely consort with such persons. These sins intrude deeply into those who are not aware of any danger and most of all, in those who have a particular affection, or more love than duty requires, for those who do not love God.

Suppose the persons with whom you fellowship are those called good people, worthy characters. Suppose them to be free from cursing, swearing, and profaneness, from sabbath-breaking and drunkenness, from lewdness of word or action, from dishonesty, lying, and slandering—entirely clear from vice of every kind. Such suppositions are hardly true. Some persons with whom you spend more time than business necessarily requires do not deserve the description of good men. They are worthy only of shame and contempt. Many of them live in open sin, in cursing and swearing, or in drunkenness or uncleanness. No one can remain ignorant of this for long, for they take little pains to hide it.

Now it is certain all vice is of an infectious nature. Who can touch tar and not be defiled? From these associations, therefore, you ought undoubtedly to flee as from the face of Satan. Otherwise, evil communication will soon corrupt your good manners.

Suppose those unholy persons with whom you frequently are friendly have no desire to communicate their own spirit to you or to induce you to follow their example. This also is a supposition that can hardly be admitted. In many cases their interest is furthered by your sharing in their sins. Everyone naturally desires, and more or less tries, to bring his friends to his own way of thinking. So, just as all good men desire and attempt to make others good like themselves, in the same way, all bad men desire and attempt to make their companions as bad as themselves. If they do not, and we allow the almost impossible supposition that they do not desire or use any efforts to bring you over to their own ways, still it is dangerous to have any intimacy with them. This applies not only to openly vicious men, but to all who do not love God, or at least fear Him and sincerely seek the kingdom of God and His righteousness.

Simply because such companions do not try to make you like themselves does not prove you are in no danger from them. Imagine a poor soul who is ill of the plague. He does not desire, he does not use the least attempt to transmit his illness to you. Yet you are careful not to touch him or go near him, so that you will not contract the same illness. To draw a parallel, suppose a man of the world has no desire, design, or aim to communicate his spiritual disorder to you. Still, do not touch him or go too near him. It is not only his reasonings and persuasions that may infect your soul, but his very presence is infectious, particularly to those who are aware of no danger.

If relating freely with worldly-minded people has no other ill effect upon you, it will surely, by imperceptible degrees, make you less heavenly minded. It will give a bias to your mind, which will continually draw your soul to earth. It will lead you, without your being conscious of it, to be again conformed to this world with its spirit, its maxims, and its vain ways. You will fall again into frivolity and the dissipation of spirit from which you had escaped.

You will soon return to excess of dress, and foolish, frothy, unprofitable associations that were abominations to you when your soul was alive to God. You will daily retreat from the simplicity of both speech and behavior that once adorned you with the doctrine of God our Savior. If you go this far in conformity to the world, you cannot expect to stop here. You will slide further in a short time. Having once lost your footing and begun to slide down, it is a thousand to one you will not stop till you come to the bottom of the hill and fall into some of those outward sins your companions commit before your eyes and in your hearing. The dread and horror that struck you at first will gradually abate, till at length you are prevailed upon to follow their example.

But suppose they do not lead you into outward sin. If they infect your spirit with pride, anger, or love of the world, it is enough. It is sufficient, without deep repentance, to drown your soul in everlasting perdition, since to be carnally minded is death.

But as dangerous as it is to become friends with men who do not know God, it is more dangerous still for men to be friendly with women of that character. Women are generally more ingratiating than men, and have far greater power of persuasion, particularly if they are pleasing in their looks or pleasing in their conversation. You must be more than human to be able to converse with them and not suffer any loss. If you do not feel any foolish or unholy desire, it is hardly possible that you will not feel an improper weakness that will make you less willing and less able to persist in the habit of denying yourself and taking up your cross daily, in the character of a good soldier of Jesus Christ.

We know that not only fornicators and adulterers but even the soft and effeminate shall have no part in the kingdom of Christ and of God. These are the consequences that will surely, though perhaps slowly, follow the mixing of Christians with those of the world. By this means, more than any other, are Christians likely to lose their strength and become like all other people.

Ironically, it is with a good plan, and from a real desire of promoting the glory of God, that many Christians enter into familiar associations with people who do not know God. They do this through a hope of awakening them from sleep and persuading them to seek essential things needed for eternal life. If, after a reasonable time and effort, you can make no impression on them, it is wise to back away and give them back to God. Otherwise, you are more likely to be harmed by them than to do them any good. If you are unable to raise their hearts up to heaven, they will draw yours down to earth. Therefore, retreat in time, come out from among them, and be separate.

Come Out From Among Them

What is the easiest and most effective method of separating ourselves from unholy men? Perhaps a few suggestions will make this plain to those who desire to know and do the will of God. First, invite no unholy person to your house except for some very particular occasion. You may think civility requires this action, and surely Christianity is no enemy to civility. Paul himself directs us to be courteous as well as sympathetic. You may be sufficiently civil, and yet keep others at a proper distance. You may be courteous in a thousand instances, and yet stand aloof. It was never Paul's purpose to recommend any courtesy that might prove a snare to the soul.

Second, never accept any invitation from an unholy person. Never pay a visit unless you wish it to be repaid. It may be that a person who desires your friendship will repeat the offer two or three times. But if you steadily refrain from accepting, he will soon become tired. It is probable he will be offended, and perhaps he will show some signs of resentment. Knowing this, you will be neither surprised nor discouraged if it happens. It is always better to please God and displease man than to please man and displease God.

Finally, you were acquainted with men of the world before you yourself knew God. What is best done to drop the company of old friends? First, allow a sufficient time to see whether you can, by argument and persuasion, induce them to follow you in the Christian path. Spare no effort. Exert all your faith and love, and plead with God in their behalf. After all that, if you cannot see that any impression is made upon them, it is your duty gently to withdraw from them and not remain entangled with them. This may be done in a short time, easily and quietly, by not returning their visits. But you must expect them to upbraid you with haughtiness and unkindness, if not to your face, then behind your back. You can accept this with a good conscience. It is the reproach of a Jesus follower.

At the age of twenty-two, when God gave me a settled conviction to be a real, rather than a nominal, Christian, my friends were as ignorant of God as I was, but there was a difference. I knew my own ignorance; they did not know theirs. I gently tried to help them, but to no avail. Meantime I found, by sad experience, that even their so-called harmless conversation dampened all my good resolutions. But how to be rid of them was the question I pondered over and over. I saw no possible way, unless it should please God to remove me to another place. This is just what He did, in a manner utterly contrary to all human probability. I was elected fellow of a different college where I knew no one. I expected that many people would come to see me, out of friendship, civility, or curiosity, and that I should have offers of friendship, new and old. But that was not what I wanted.

Entering into this new situation, I resolved to have no acquaintance by chance—only by choice. I would choose only those I had reason to believe would help me on my way to heaven. Because of this, I carefully observed the temper and behavior of all who visited me. I saw no reason to think that most of these truly loved or feared God. Therefore, I did not choose them for acquaintances. I did not expect them to help my spiritual growth. Therefore, when any of these came to see me, I behaved as courteously as I could. When asked to return the visit, I gave no answer. When they had come a few more times and found I still declined returning their visits, they ceased coming. This has been my invariable rule for almost sixty years. I knew many reproaches would follow, but that did not deter me, as I knew full well it was my calling to receive both evil report and good report.

I earnestly advise all of you who wish to be complete Christians to adopt the same plan, however contrary it may seem to social custom. Closely observe which of those you meet believe as you do. Notice those you have reason to believe fear God and are seeking righteousness. Those are worthy of your acquaintance. Gladly and freely have fellowship with them at all opportunities. Gently and quietly drop all who do not have that character. However good-natured and knowledgeable those may be, they can do you no real service. If they do not lead you into outward sin, they will be a continual clog to your soul, and will hinder your running with vigor and cheerfulness the spiritual race set before you.

If any of your Christian friends turn away from the holy commandment once delivered to them, use every prudent method to bring them back to the right path. Then if you cannot prevail, let them go. Keep commending them to God in prayer, but, to save your own soul, drop all intimacy with them.

I also advise you to walk cautiously with your own family. You must certainly be friendly with parents, whether Christian or not, if they desire it, and with your brothers and sisters, especially if they want your service. You are not under any such obligation with respect to your more distant relations. Courtesy and natural affection may require that you visit them sometimes. But if they neither know nor seek God, it should certainly be as seldom as possible. When you are with them, you should not stay a day longer than decency requires. Again, whoever you are with at any time, remember Paul's solemn caution: "Let no corrupt communication proceed out of your mouth, but that which is good to the use of edifying, that it may minister grace unto the hearers" (Eph. 4:29).

We have no authority to vary from this rule without grieving the Holy Spirit. If you keep closely to it, those who are not Christian will soon avoid your company. So all who fear or love God should come out from among all those who do neither. In a plain scriptural sense, Christians should be separate from them and any unnecessary relationship with them. "Touch not," saith the Lord, "the unclean thing," or person, any more than necessity requires, "and I will receive you" into the household of God. "And I will be a Father unto you," will embrace you with paternal affection, "and ye shall be my sons and daughters, saith the Lord Almighty."

The promise is plain to all who renounce the company of ungodly men. God pledges to give them all the blessings He has prepared for His beloved children, both in time and eternity. Let all who have any regard for the favor and blessings of God beware of any friendship, or form any connection with ungodly men, more than necessary business requires. With all possible speed, break off all such relationships already contracted, and all such connections already formed. Let no pleasure resulting from such acquaintance, no gain found or expected from such connections, be of any consideration when balanced against a clear, positive command of God. In such a case, tear away the most pleasing friend and cast him from you. Give up all thought and design of renewing the relationship. Absolutely renounce the most profitable connection and cast it from you. It is better for you to experience life alone than to be cast into hellfire.

12

Working Out Our Own Salvation

Work out your own salvation with fear and trembling. For it is God that worketh in you both to will and to do of his good pleasure. (Philippians 2:12–13)

Some great truths, such as the existence and character of God and the difference between moral good and evil, were known even in the heathen world. Traces of these truths are found in all nations. In some sense it may be said God has showed all of us what is good, just and merciful, and how to walk humbly with Him. He has, in some measure, shown everyone there is an unwritten law within themselves. They show the work and substance of the law written in their hearts by God, who also wrote the commandments on stone. Their conscience bears them witness whether they act according to His law.

However, two great doctrines contain many truths of the most important nature, of which all heathens have been totally ignorant. These are the doctrines that relate to the eternal Jesus and the Holy Spirit.

Jesus gave himself to be an atonement for the sins of the world, and the Holy Spirit renews men into the image in

---

Taken from John Wesley's, *Sermons on Several Occasions*, "Working Out Our Own Salvation," XC, Vol. 2, p. 233 ff.

which they were originally created. Many have attempted to find some resemblance of those truths in the immense writings of heathen authors, but the resemblance is extremely faint and is mostly imagined. Furthermore, even this faint resemblance has been found only in the writings of a few, and those were the most advanced men of their generations. The multitudes that surrounded them had little knowledge from the philosophers, and remained totally ignorant of these great truths. Certainly these truths were never known to the bulk of mankind until they were revealed by Jesus' gospel.

Notwithstanding any spark of knowledge glimmering here and there, the whole earth was covered with darkness until the Sun of righteousness arose and scattered the night. Since then, a great light has shined. Thousands in every age have known that God so loved the world that He gave His only Son so that whoever believed in Him should not perish but have everlasting life. Being aware of God's Scripture, they have known that God has also given us His Holy Spirit, who works in us both to will and to do of His ways.

How remarkable are Paul's words concerning Christ Jesus:

> Who, being in the form of God, thought it not robbery to be equal with God. But made himself of no reputation, and took upon him the form of a servant, and was made in the likeness of men: And being found in fashion as a man, he humbled himself, and became obedient unto death. (Phil. 2:6–8)

This scripture implies both the fullness and the supreme height of the Godhead. Opposite it are the two thoughts: "took upon him" (or emptied) and "humbled." Jesus emptied himself of that divine fullness, veiled His fullness from the eyes of men and angels, taking the form of a servant to be made in the likeness of man. By that very act of taking on the likeness of a real man, like other men, He emptied himself. Being made like a common man, without any particular beauty or excellence, He humbled himself to an even greater degree, becoming obedient to God, though equal with Him, even to death on the cross, the greatest example ever of humiliation and obedience.

Having shown Jesus' example, Paul warns all to secure the salvation that Jesus purchased for them: "Work out your own salvation with fear and trembling. For it is God which worketh in you both to will and to do of his good pleasure."

In these words we may observe three things. First, and most important, it is *God who works in us* both to will and to do of His ways. Second, *we work out* our own salvation with fear and trembling. Finally, the connection between them is that it is God who works in us *both to will and to do*, and we work out our own salvation through His grace.

The meaning of these words may be made more clear by transposition. It is God who of His good pleasure works in you both to will and to do. This position of the words connecting "of his good pleasure" with the word "works" removes all imagination of merit from man, and gives God all the glory of His work. Otherwise, we might have some room for boasting as if it were something done by us that first moved God to work. Paul's expression cuts off all vain conceits, clearly showing God's motive to work lies wholly in himself. It is by His own grace and unmerited mercy. By this alone God is impelled to work in man both to will and to do.

This scripture is capable of two interpretations, both of which are true. First, "to will" includes the whole of the inward man; "to do," the whole of the outward. Properly understood, this implies it is God who works both inward and outward holiness. "To will" may imply every good desire; "to do," whatever results from that desire. Then the sentence means God breathes into us every good desire, and brings every good desire to good effect. The original Greek seems to favor this construction. "To will" plainly includes every good desire, whether relating to our tempers, words, or actions, in inward or outward holiness. "To do" clearly implies all that power from on high, all that energy working every right disposition in us, and then furnishing us for every good word and work. Nothing can so directly strip pride from man as a deep, lasting conviction of this. When we become thoroughly aware that we have nothing that is not a gift, we cannot glory as if we earned it. If we know and feel that all good in us is from above, as well as the power conducting us to the good end, and know God not only infuses every good desire but accompanies and follows it lest we lose it, then it clearly follows that any who glory must glory in the Lord.

The second point is, if God works in you, then you work out your own salvation. The original word rendered "work out" means doing a thing thoroughly. "Your own" means it is personal and you must do this yourself or it will be forever undone.

Salvation begins with what is usually and properly termed preventing grace. This includes one's first wish to please God. It is the first dawn of light acknowledging His will, along with the first slight fleeting conviction of having sinned against Him. All these imply some degree of salvation, and the beginning of a deliverance from an unfeeling heart, which had been quite ignorant of God and His ways.

Salvation is carried on by convincing grace, which Scripture usually terms repentance. With this comes a larger measure of self-knowledge, and a greater deliverance from a stony heart. Later we experience the proper Christian salvation where we are saved by faith through grace, which consists of two divisions, justification and sanctification. By justification, we are saved from the guilt of sin and restored to the favor of God. By sanctification, we are saved from the power and root of sin and restored to the image of God.

Experience as well as Scripture show this salvation to be paradoxically instantaneous and gradual. It begins the moment we are justified, in the holy, humble, gentle, patient love of God and man. It gradually increases from that moment, like a grain of mustard seed that at first is the least of all seeds. Afterward it puts forth large branches and becomes a great tree until, in another instant, the heart is cleansed from all sin and filled with pure love to God and man. Even that love increases more and more until we grow up in all things to Him who is our head, until we attain the measure of the stature of the fullness of Jesus.

Next, how are we to work out this salvation? Paul asserts, "With fear and trembling." There is another passage of his, in Ephesians, in which the same expression occurs, which gives light to this one. He tells servants to obey their masters according to the present state of things, remaining fully aware that soon the servant will be free from his master (Eph. 6:5). This is a proverbial, not a literal, expression. What master could bear, much less require, a servant to stand trembling and quaking before him? Paul's following words exclude this meaning. He is speaking of singleness of heart, a single eye to the will and providence of God. It is not the eye of man-pleasing service, but as a servant of Christ, doing the will of God from the heart. It is doing all things as the will of God with all one's might.

It is easy to see that these strong expressions clearly imply two things. First, everything must be done with total earnestness of spirit, care, and caution. Second, it must be done with complete diligence, speed, punctuality, and exactness. How easily may we transfer this to the business of life, the working out of our own salvation. With the same disposition and in the same manner that Christian servants serve their masters on earth, let them also labor to serve their Master who is in heaven. It is to be done with the utmost earnestness of spirit, with all possible care and caution, and with the utmost diligence, speed, punctuality, and exactness.

Here are the steps Scripture directs us to take in working out our own salvation. Isaiah gives a general answer, mentioning the first steps we are to take: "Cease to do evil; learn to do well" (1:16–17). To have God work in you that faith from which comes both present and eternal salvation, through grace already given, flee from all sin, carefully avoiding every evil word and work, and abstain from all appearance of evil.

Learn to do well, be zealous in good works—works of piety

as well as works of mercy—family prayer, and praying to God in secret. Fast in secret, and your Father who sees in secret will reward you openly. Search the Scriptures. Hear them in public, read them in private, and meditate on them. At every opportunity, partake of the Lord's Supper, in remembrance of Him, and He will meet you at His own table. Fellowship with God's children, under grace. As you can, do good to the souls and bodies of all people. In this, be steadfast and unmovable, always abounding in the work of God.

Then it only remains for you to deny yourself, taking up your cross daily. Deny yourself everything that does not contribute to your pleasing God. Willingly embrace every means of drawing near to God, even if it is a cross, and grievous to you. When you have redemption in the blood of Jesus, you will go on to perfection. Then, walking in the light as He is in the light, you are enabled to testify that He is faithful and just. Not only does He forgive your sins, but He also cleanses you from all unrighteousness.

Some have difficulty understanding this verse in light of Phil. 2:12. It appears the two are in opposition. Because it is God who works in us both to will and to do, there seems no need of our working. Does His working in us eliminate the necessity of our working at all, making our working impracticable as well as unnecessary? If we agree that God does all, what is there left for us to do? This is human reasoning.

At first, this appears extremely plausible. But it is not, as is evident when we consider the matter more. We shall then see there is no tension between "God works; therefore, do ye work." On the contrary, there is close connection in two respects. First, God works; therefore you can work. Second, God works; therefore you must work. Because God works in you, you can work; otherwise it would be impossible. If He did not work, it would be impossible for you to work out your own salvation. Jesus told us it is impossible for a rich man to enter into the kingdom of heaven; but the same is true for any man unless God works in him.

By nature, all men are not only sick but dead in trespasses and in sins. It is not possible for them to do anything well until God raises them from the dead. It was impossible for Lazarus to come forth from the dead until the Lord had given him life. It is equally impossible for us to come out of our sins, or make the least motion toward it, until God stirs our dead souls into life. This gives no excuse to those who continue in sin and lay the blame on God by saying He must quicken us, for we cannot do it ourselves. Although souls of men are dead in sin by nature, no one, unless he somehow quenched the Spirit, is wholly empty of the grace of God. No man living is entirely devoid of natural conscience. What is called natural is better called "preventing grace." Everyone has a measure of this, which man cannot stop. Sooner or later, everyone has some good intentions, although most stifle them before they can produce deep results. Everyone has some measure of that light, some faint glimmering ray of decency, which sooner or later, more or less, enlightens everyone. Everyone, except one of that small number whose consciences are numb, feels uneasy when acting contrary to the light of his own conscience. So it is, *no one sins for lack of grace, but only because the grace given is not used.*

So it is because God works in you, you are now able to work out your own salvation. Since He works in you of His own good pleasure, without any merit of yours, both to will and to do, it becomes possible for you to fulfill all righteousness. It is possible for you to love God because He has first loved you, and to walk in love after the pattern of Jesus. We know His Word to be absolutely true—without Him we can do nothing.

On the other hand, every believer can say, "I can do all things through Christ which strengtheneth me" (Phil. 4:13). Always remember that God has joined grace and works together in the experience of every believer. We must remain careful not to think they are to be pulled apart. We must beware of mock humility that teaches us to excuse our willful disobedience, saying we can do nothing, without once mentioning God's grace. Think again. Reconsider what you say.

If it is really true you can do nothing, then you have no faith. If you have no faith, you are in a wretched condition, outside the state of salvation. You can always do something through Christ's strengthening you. By prayer stir up the spark of grace which is now in you, and He will give you more grace. God works in you; therefore you must work. You must work together with Him, otherwise He will cease working. The general rule on which His grace proceeds is this: unto him who has, more shall be given, but from him who has not, who does not improve the grace already given, what he assuredly has shall be taken away. Even Augustine, who is generally thought to believe the opposite doctrine, remarks that God who made us with our personality will not save us without our personality.

God will not save us unless we attempt to save ourselves, and fight the good fight of faith to lay hold of eternal life. Unless we struggle to enter in at the straight gate, deny ourselves, take up our cross daily, and work by every possible means to assure our own calling and divine choice, we will lose what we have. Strive, then, brothers and sisters, not for that which perishes, but for that which endures to everlasting life. Say with our blessed Jesus, "My Father worketh hitherto, and I work" (John 5:17).

Knowing that He still works in you, never weary of well doing. In virtue of the grace of God, preventing, accompanying, and following you, go on in the work of faith, the patience of hope, and the labor of love. Be steadfast, always abounding in the work of the Lord. And the God of peace, who brought again from the dead our Lord Jesus, that great Shepherd of the sheep, make you perfect in every good work to do His will. May He work in you what is well pleasing in His sight, through Jesus Christ, to whom be glory forever and ever!

13

A Call to Backsliders

Will the Lord cast off for ever? and will he be favourable no more? Is his mercy clean gone for ever? doth his promise fail for evermore? (Psalm 77:7, 8)

Presumption is a great snare in which many are caught. Some presume so much mercy from God that they forget His justice. Although the Bible expressly declares that without holiness no man shall see the Lord (Heb. 12:14), they still presume that in the end, God will be different than His Word. Too many imagine they may live and die in sin, yet still escape God's judgment.

While many are destroyed by presumption, there are still more who perish because of despair and lack of hope. They think it impossible to escape destruction. Having many times fought against their spiritual enemies, and having always been overcome, they stop their efforts. They fight no more, lacking hope of victory. Knowing by melancholy experience that they have no power in themselves to help themselves, and having no hope for God's help, they lie down under the burden. They no longer strive, thinking it is impossible to attain sinlessness.

Taken from John Wesley's, *Sermons on Several Occasions*, "A Call to Backsliders," XCI, Vol. 2, p. 239 ff.

In all these cases, each heart knows its own bitterness. It is not easy for others to understand if they have never felt it. Who can know the things of a person but his own spirit? Who knows, except by personal experience, what this sort of wounded spirit means? Consequently, few know how to empathize with those who are under the temptation to cease striving. Only a few have duly considered this and fewer still are not deceived by appearances. Seeing people continuing in sin, they assume that is a result of mere arrogance. In reality, it is from the contrary principle of despair. Either they have no hope at all, so they do not strive at all; or else they have some times of hope, and while that lasts, strive for mastery. But that hope soon fails. Once again they cease to strive, and are taken captive by Satan.

This is often the case with those who began to run well but soon tired on the heavenly road. This is particularly so with those who once saw the glory of God in the face of Jesus Christ but afterward grieved His Holy Spirit and shipwrecked their faith. Indeed, many of these rush into sin as a dog on chase. They sin so high-handedly as to utterly quench the Holy Spirit of God. He gives them up to their own lusts, and lets them follow their own imaginations. Those who are thus given up remain quite ignorant, without either fear or sorrow or care, utterly at ease and unconcerned about God or heaven or hell. Satan contributes to this by blinding and hardening their hearts. But still, even these would not be so careless were it not for despair. The great reason they have no sorrow or care is because they have no hope. They honestly believe they have provoked God and can no longer petition Him.

Yet we should not utterly give up even on these. We have known some, even the most careless, whom God has visited again and restored to himself. We can have much more hope for backsliders who are not careless but remain uneasy, wanting to escape out of Satan's snare, while thinking it is impossible. They are convinced they cannot save themselves, but believe God will not save them. They believe He has irrevocably shut up His lovingkindness in displeasure. They reinforce themselves, believing this for many reasons. Until their reasons are clearly removed, they cannot hope for deliverance.

It is in order to relieve those hopeless, helpless souls that I propose to explore the main reasons why so many backsliders cast away hope, and suppose that God has forgotten their name. I wish to give a clear and full answer to each of those reasons.

Why Backsliders Remain Backslidden

Here are the main explanations as to why so many backsliders think God has forgotten to be gracious. I do not say these are all the reasons. There may be many others hidden in their own hearts. I will deal only with the most plausible and common causes.

The first argument that persuades many backsliders to believe the Lord will no longer be petitioned is this: "If," they say, "a man rebels against an earthly king, many times he dies for the first offense; he loses his life for the first transgression. If, possibly, the crime is extenuated by some favorable circumstances, or if strong intercession is made for him, his life may be spared. But if, after a full and free pardon, he were guilty of rebelling a second time, who would dare to intercede for him? He must expect no further mercy. Now, if one rebelling against an earthly king, after he has been freely pardoned once, cannot reasonably hope to be forgiven a second time, what must happen to him who, after having been freely pardoned for rebelling against the great King of heaven and earth, rebels against Him again? What can be expected but that vengeance will come upon him to the fullest?"

This argument, drawn from reason, is then enforced by several passages of Scripture. One of the strongest of these occurs in John's first letter: "If any man see his brother sin a sin which is not unto death, he shall ask, and he [God] shall give him life for them that sin not unto death. There is a sin unto death: I do not say that he shall pray for it" (1 John 5:16).

Therefore they argue, "Certainly 'I do not say that he shall pray for it' is the same as 'I say he shall not pray for it.' So Paul considers one who has committed this sin to be in a desperate state indeed. His situation is so desperate that we may not even pray for his forgiveness, or ask life for him, and what may we more reasonably imagine to be a sin unto death than a willful rebellion after a full and free pardon.

"Consider," they continue, "those terrible passages in the letter to the Hebrews, one in the sixth chapter and one in the tenth. To begin with the latter, 'If we sin wilfully after that we have received the knowledge of the truth, there remaineth no more sacrifice for sins, but a certain fearful looking for of judgment and fiery indignation, which shall devour the adversaries. He that despised Moses' law died without mercy. . . . Of how much sorer punishment, suppose ye, shall he be thought worthy, who hath trodden under foot the Son of God, and hath counted the blood of the covenant, wherewith he was sanctified, an unholy thing, and hath done despite unto the Spirit of grace? For we know him that hath said, Vengeance belongeth unto me, I will recompense, saith the Lord. . . . It is a fearful thing to fall into the hands of the living God' (Heb. 10:26–31). Now it is expressly declared here by the Holy Spirit that our case is desperate. It is declared that if, after we have received the knowledge of truth, after we have experienced it, we sin willfully, which we have undoubtedly done over and over, there remains no other sacrifice for sin but a certain fearful looking for of judgment and fiery indignation that shall devour the adversaries.

"And that passage in the sixth chapter is exactly parallel. 'It is impossible for those who were once enlightened, and have tasted of the heavenly gift, and were made partakers of the Holy Ghost,' if they have fallen away, 'to renew them again unto repentance; seeing they crucify to themselves the Son of God afresh, and put him to an open shame' (Heb. 6:4,

6))." Some think the words "it is impossible" are not to be taken literally as meaning absolute impossibility, but meaning with great difficulty. We do not have sufficient reason to depart from the literal meaning, because it neither implies absurdity nor contradicts other scriptures. "Then does this not cut off all hope," they ask, "as we have undoubtedly tasted of that heavenly gift and been made partakers of the Holy Spirit? How is it possible to renew us again to repentance, to an entire change both of heart and life, if we have crucified to ourselves the Son of God afresh, and put Him to an open shame?"

A still more fearful passage is in the twelfth chapter of Matthew. "All manner of sin and blasphemy shall be forgiven unto men: but the blasphemy against the Holy Ghost shall not be forgiven unto men. And whosoever speaketh a word against the Son of Man, it shall be forgiven him: but whosoever speaketh against the Holy Ghost, it shall not be forgiven him, neither in this world, nor in the world to come" (Matt. 12:31–32). Exactly parallel to these are the words of our Lord, which are stated by Mark, "Verily I say unto you, All sins shall be forgiven unto the sons of men, and blasphemies wherewith soever they shall blaspheme: But he that shall blaspheme against the Holy Ghost hath never forgiveness, but is in danger of eternal damnation" (Mark 3:28–29).

In the opinion of some, all these passages point to the same sin. Not only the words of Jesus, but also those of John, concerning the "sin unto death," and those of Paul, concerning crucifying "to themselves the Son of God afresh" (Heb. 6:6), treading underfoot the Son of God, and doing "despite to the Spirit of grace" (Heb. 10:29), all refer to the blasphemy against the Holy Spirit, the only sin that shall never be forgiven. Whether they do or not, it must be agreed that this blasphemy is absolutely unpardonable, and that for those who have been guilty of this, God will no longer be entreated.

To confirm those arguments drawn from reason and from Scripture, they appeal to fact. They ask, "Is it not a fact that those who fall away from justifying grace, who make shipwreck of the faith, that faith from which present salvation comes, die without mercy? How much less can any of those escape, who fall away from sanctifying grace, who make shipwreck of that faith that cleansed them from all pollution of flesh and spirit? Has there ever been an instance of one or the other of these being renewed again to repentance?"

These are the usual arguments drawn from reason, from Scripture, and from fact, whereby backsliders are apt to justify themselves in casting away hope because they imagine God has utterly shut up His lovingkindness by displeasure. I have proposed these arguments in their full strength that we may form better judgment concerning them, and see whether each may not receive a clear, full, satisfactory answer.

God's Mercy Toward Backsliders

Let us begin with the backslider's first argument. "If a man rebel against an earthly prince, he may possibly be forgiven the first time. But if, after a full and free pardon, he should rebel again, there is no hope of obtaining a second pardon. He must expect to die without mercy. Now if he who rebels again against an earthly king can look for no second pardon, how can he look for mercy who rebels a second time against the great King of heaven?"

This argument drawn from the analogy between earthly and heavenly things is plausible, but it is not solid for this obvious reason. Analogy has no place here. There can be no analogy or proportion between the mercy of men and that of God. "To whom then will ye liken me or shall I be equal? saith the Holy One" (Isa. 40:25). Unto whom in either heaven or earth? Who is he among the gods that shall be compared unto the Lord? "I have said, Ye are gods" (Ps. 82:6), the psalmist said, speaking of supreme rulers. Such is your dignity and power compared to common men. But what are they to the God of heaven? As a bubble on the wave. What is their power compared to His power? What is their mercy compared to His mercy? Therefore, we have that assuring word, "I am God and not man, therefore the house of Israel is not consumed." Because He is God and not man, His compassions do not fail. None then can infer that because an earthly king will not pardon one who rebels against him a second time, that the King of heaven will not.

God forgives not only seven times but seventy times seven. If your rebellions were multiplied as the stars of heaven, if they were more in number than the hairs on your head, yet "return unto the Lord, and he will have mercy upon [you]; and to our God, for he will abundantly pardon" (Isa. 55:7).

"But does not John cut us off from this hope by what he says of the 'sin unto death'? Is not 'I do not say that he shall pray for it' the same as 'I say he shall not pray for it'? Doesn't this imply that God has determined not to hear that prayer, that He will not give life to such a sinner, even through the prayer of a righteous man?"

"I do not say that he shall pray for it" certainly means he shall not pray for it. And it doubtless implies that God will not give life to those who have sinned this sin. Their sentence is passed, and God has determined it shall not be revoked. It cannot be altered even by earnest, effective prayer, which in other cases brings benefit.

What is the "sin unto death," and what is the death which is fixed to it? Many years ago, I was with a group of Christians who were more experienced in spiritual things than any I had ever met. I asked them what they understood by the sin unto death, mentioned in John's first letter. They answered, "If anyone is sick among us, he sends for the elders of the church, and they pray over him, and the prayer of faith saves the sick and the Lord raises him up. If he has committed sins, which God was punishing by that sickness, they are forgiven. But sometimes none of us can pray that God would raise him up. We are obliged to tell him, 'We are afraid that you have sinned a sin unto death, a sin which God has determined to punish with death. We cannot pray for your recovery.' And we have never yet known an instance of such a person recovering."

I see nothing wrong in this interpretation of the word. It is one meaning, at least, of the expression "a sin unto death," a sin that God has determined to punish by the death of the sinner. If, therefore, one has sinned a sin of this kind, and the sin has overtaken the person, if God is chastising by some severe disease, it will not help to pray for life. That one is irrevocably sentenced to die. But this has no reference to eternal death, and does not imply the sinner is condemned to die the second death. It implies the contrary. The body is destroyed that the soul may escape destruction.

I have, during the course of many years, known many sinners whom God has cut short in the midst of their journey, before they had lived out half their days. These were mainly notorious backsliders who had fallen from high degrees of holiness, those who had given many occasions for enemies of religion to blaspheme. These, I believe, had sinned a sin unto death, in consequence of which they were cut off, sometimes more swiftly, sometimes more slowly, in an unexpected way. But in most of these cases, mercy rejoiced over judgment. The persons themselves were fully convinced of the goodness as well as justice of God. They acknowledged that He destroyed the body in order to save the soul. Before they died, God healed their backsliding. So they died that they might live forever.

A very remarkable instance of this occurred years ago. A young coal miner in Kingswood, near Bristol, was an eminent sinner, and afterward an eminent saint. Little by little, he renewed his acquaintance with his old companions, who, by degrees, worked on him until he dropped all his faith and was twice as much a child of hell as before. One day he was working in the pit with a serious young man, who suddenly stopped and cried out, "Oh, Tommy, what a man you once were! How your works and example inspired many to love and to good works! And what are you now? What would become of you if you were to die as you are?"

"Nay, God forbid," said Thomas, "for then I should fall headlong into hell! Oh, let us pray to God!"

They did so for a long time, first one, and then the other. They called upon God with strong cries and tears, wrestling with Him in mighty prayer. After some time, Thomas broke out, "Now I know God has healed my backsliding. I know, again, that my Redeemer lives, and that He has washed me from my sins with His own blood. I am willing to go to Him."

Instantly part of the pit caved in, crushing him to death. Whoever you are who has sinned a sin unto death, take this to heart. It may be God will require your soul at a moment when you do not expect it. But if He does, there is mercy in the midst of judgment. You shall not die eternally.

"But what do you say to that other scripture, namely Hebrews 10? Does that leave any hope to notorious backsliders that they shall not die eternally, that they can ever recover the favor of God, or escape the damnation of hell? 'If we sin willfully after we have received the knowledge of the truth, there remaineth no more sacrifice for sins, but a certain fearful looking for of judgment and fiery indignation, which shall devour the adversaries. He that despised Moses' law died without mercy. . . . Of how much sorer punishment, suppose ye, shall he be thought worthy, who hath trodden under foot the Son of God, and hath counted the blood of the covenant wherewith he was sanctified, an unholy thing, and hath done despite unto the Spirit of grace?' And isn't the desperate, irrecoverable state of willful backsliders fully confirmed by the parallel passage in the sixth chapter? 'It is impossible for those who were once enlightened . . . and made partakers of the Holy Ghost . . . if they shall fall away, to renew them again unto repentance; seeing they crucify to themselves the Son of God afresh, and put him to an open shame.' "

These passages seem to me parallel to each other, and deserve deep consideration. In order to understand them, it will be necessary to identify the persons spoken of here and the sin they committed, which made their case nearly, if not quite, desperate.

It is clear to all who consider and compare both these passages that the persons spoken of here are only those who have been justified. They were given understanding and enlightened to see the light of the glory of God in the face of Jesus Christ. These only have tasted of the heavenly gift: remission of sins. They were made partakers both of the witness and the fruit of the Holy Spirit. This statement cannot be applied to any but those who have been justified.

They had been sanctified, at least in the first degree, as are all who receive remission of sins. So the passage in Hebrews 10 states expressly, "[He] hath counted the blood of the covenant, wherewith he was sanctified, an unholy thing."

This scripture, then, concerns only those who have been justified, and at least in part sanctified. Therefore all who never were enlightened with the light of the glory of God in this way and never received remission of sins, or received the Holy Spirit, were never Christians and are not concerned here. Whatever other passages of Scripture may condemn the unsaved, it is certain they are not condemned by either the sixth or the tenth chapters of Hebrews. Both of those chapters speak wholly and solely of the ones who have forsaken the faith, which the lost never did. It was not possible for them to lose it, for one cannot lose what was never had. Therefore, whatever judgments are denounced in these scriptures, they are not denounced against sinners.

Next we ask, What was the sin of the persons described here? In order to understand this, we should remember that whenever the Jews prevailed on a Christian to forsake the faith, they required him to declare, in express terms, and in the public assembly, that Jesus was a deceiver of the people, and that He had suffered the punishment that His crimes justly deserved. This is the sin that Paul in Hebrews 6 terms emphatically, falling away and crucifying Jesus again, putting Him to an open shame. This is what he calls in Hebrews 10 counting the blood of the covenant an unholy thing, treading underfoot the Son of God, and being contemptuous of the Spirit of grace.

Now, who has fallen away like this? Which of you has crucified the Son of God afresh in this manner? Not one, nor has one of you put Him to this open shame. If you had formally renounced that only sacrifice for sin, no other sacrifice would remain, so that you must have perished without mercy. But this is not your case. Not one of you has renounced that sacrifice by which the Son of God made a full and perfect payment for the sins of the whole world. Bad as you may be, you shudder at the thought. Therefore Jesus' sacrifice still remains effective for you. Cast away needless fears and come boldly to the throne of grace. The way is still open for backsliders to again obtain mercy and find grace in time of need.

"But the well-known words of our Lord himself cut us off from all hope of mercy. He says, 'All manner of sin and blasphemy shall be forgiven unto men: but the blasphemy against the Holy Ghost shall not be forgiven unto men. And whosoever speaketh a word against the Son of man, it shall be forgiven him: but whosoever speaketh against the Holy Ghost, it shall not be forgiven him, neither in this world, neither in the world to come.' Therefore, if we have been guilty of this sin, there can be no room for mercy. The very same thing is repeated by Mark, in almost the same words. 'Verily I say unto you' (a solemn preface, always indicating the great importance of what follows), 'All sins shall be forgiven unto the sons of men, and blasphemies wherewith soever they shall blaspheme: But he that shall blaspheme against the Holy Ghost hath never forgiveness, but is in danger of eternal damnation.' "

An immense number of Christians have been more or less distressed because of this scripture. Many have been greatly perplexed by it. Most who are truly convinced of sin, and seriously try to save their souls, have felt some uneasiness for fear they had committed, or might commit, this unpardonable sin. Frequently their uneasiness increased because they could not find anyone to comfort them about this scripture. Their acquaintances, even the most religious, had no more understanding of the matter than themselves, and they could not find teachers who had written satisfactorily on this scripture.

There was never more proof of the smallness of human understanding, even in those who have honest hearts and seek the truth. It seems impossible that anyone who studies this for one hour can remain in doubt about it when our Lord himself, in the very passage cited above, has so clearly told us what that blasphemy is. "He that shall blaspheme against the Holy Ghost hath never forgiveness . . . because they said, He hath an unclean spirit" (Mark 3:29–30). This, then, and this alone, if we allow our Lord to understand His own meaning, is the blasphemy against the Holy Spirit. It is saying that Jesus had an unclean spirit, affirming that Christ worked His miracles by the power of an evil spirit, or, more particularly, that He cast out devils "by Beelzebub, the prince of devils" (Matt. 12:24).

Now, have you been guilty of this? Who has affirmed that He cast out devils by the prince of devils? You have feared where there is no cause for it. Dismiss that fear and be more rational in the future. Fear submitting to pride, fear yielding to anger, fear loving the world and the things of the world, fear foolish and sinful desires, but never again be afraid of committing blasphemy against the Holy Spirit. You are in no more danger of doing this than of pulling the sun from the sky.

You have then no reason from Scripture for imagining that the Lord has forgotten to be merciful. The arguments drawn from it, you see, have no value, are utterly inconclusive. Is there any more importance in what has been learned from experience or matter of fact?

This point may be precisely proved with total certainty. Some may ask, "Do any who have really renounced their faith find mercy from God? Do any who have made shipwreck of faith and a good conscience recover what they have lost? Do you know, have you ever seen any instance of persons who found redemption in the blood of Jesus, and afterward fell away, and yet were restored, 'renewed again to repentance'?"

I do. I know of not merely one, or a hundred, but several thousand. In every place where the arm of the Lord has been revealed, and many sinners converted to God, there are several who turn away from His holy ways. For most of these, it would have been better if they had never known His way of righteousness. That only increased their damnation since they die in their sins. However, there are others who remember Him whom they have rejected and mourn, refusing to be comforted. Then, sooner or later, He again lifts the light of His countenance upon them. He lifts their heads that hang down, and firms their feeble souls. He restores them so they can say, "My soul doth magnify the Lord, and my spirit hath rejoiced in God my Saviour" (Luke 1:46–47).

There are numberless instances of those who had fallen, but now stand straight. In fact, it is far more common for a believer to fall and be restored than it is for a believer to never backslide before being established in stable faith. Again, some will ask, "But have any that had fallen from sanctifying grace been restored to the blessing they had lost?" This also is a point of experience, and I repeat my observations during many years, from one end of the land to the other.

First, there have been many persons of every age and sex who have given all the proofs that they were sanctified through being cleansed from all pollution of both flesh and spirit. They loved the Lord their God with all their heart, mind, soul, and strength, and continually presented their souls as a living sacrifice, holy and acceptable to God. They rejoiced evermore, prayed without ceasing, and in everything gave thanks. This is what I believe to be true, scriptural sanctification.

Second, it is usual for those who are sanctified to believe they cannot fall, supposing themselves pillars in the temple of God that shall never go out. Nevertheless, we have seen some of the strongest of them, after a time, removed from their steadfastness. Sometimes suddenly, but more often by slow degrees, they have yielded to temptation. Then pride, or anger, or foolish desires have again sprung up in their hearts. Sometimes they utterly lost the life of God, and sin regained dominion over them.

Yet, several of these, after being thoroughly aware of their fall, were deeply ashamed before God. Having once again regained His love, they were perfected, established, strengthened, and settled in it. They again received their previous blessing, with abundant increase. It is remarkable that many who had so deeply fallen either from justifying or from sanctifying grace that they could hardly be ranked among the servants of God, have been restored, frequently in an instant, to all that they had lost. But that seldom occurred until they had been shaken over the mouth of hell. At once, they recovered both a consciousness of His favor and the experience of the pure love of God. In one moment they received anew remission of sins and a place among the sanctified.

But let not any man infer from this that God has given anyone a license to sin. Neither let any dare to continue in sin because of demonstrable instances of extraordinary mercy. That is a most desperate and irrational presumption that leads to utter, irrecoverable destruction. In all my experience, I have not known one who continued in sin by a presumption that God would save him at the last, who was not miserably disappointed, dying in his sins. To turn the grace of God into an encouragement to sin is the sure way into hell.

It is not for these desperate children of the world that the preceding assurances are given. These are for all whose remembrance of their sins is grievous, and the burden of them is intolerable. Set before these is an open door of hope. They may go in and give thanks to the Lord. They can know that the Lord is gracious and merciful, longsuffering, and of great goodness.

See how high the heavens are from the earth. That is how far He will move their sins from them. He is not always chiding, nor does He stay angry forever. Say it in your heart,

"I will give all for all." Your offering will be accepted. Give Him all your heart. Let all that is within you continually cry out, "You are my God, and I will thank you. You are my God, and I will praise you. This God is my God forever and ever. He shall be my guide even unto death."

14

The More Excellent Way

Covet earnestly the best gifts: and yet I shew unto you a more excellent way. (1 Corinthians 12:31)

In the verses preceding this scripture, Paul spoke of the extraordinary gifts of the Holy Spirit, such as healing the sick, prophesying (that is, foretelling things to come), speaking with strange tongues (such as the speaker had never learned), and the miraculous interpretation of tongues. Paul calls these gifts desirable. He exhorts all the Corinthians to covet them earnestly, so by these gifts they might be better qualified to be more useful to both Christians and heathens. "And yet," he says, "shew I unto you a more excellent way." There is something far more desirable than all these put together, and it always leads to happiness both in this world and the world to come. On the other hand, one might have all those other gifts to the highest degree, and yet be miserable both now and for eternity.

It does not appear that these extraordinary gifts of the Holy Spirit were common in the church for more than two or three centuries. We seldom hear of them after that fatal period when Emperor Constantine called himself a Christian

Taken from John Wesley's, *Sermons on Several Occasions*, "The More Excellent Way," XCIV, Vol. 2, p. 266 ff.

and, from a fruitless idea of promoting the Christian cause, heaped riches, power, and honor on Christians in general, but most especially on the Christian clergy. After that, these gifts almost totally ceased. Very few instances of them were recorded. The cause of this was not, as some suppose, because there was no more need for them since all the world had become Christian. This idea is a miserable mistake. Not a twentieth part of the world was even nominally Christian.

The real reason those extraordinary gifts were lost was that the love of God in almost all so-called Christians had grown cold. Christians had no more of the Spirit of Christ than the other heathens had. Jesus, when He examined His church, could hardly find faith upon the earth. This was the real reason why the gifts of the Holy Spirit were no longer found in the Christian Church. The Christians had turned heathens again, and had only a dead form of worship left.

However, we are not now examining the extraordinary gifts. We are discussing the ordinary gifts. These, too, we may covet earnestly in order to be more useful to God in our generation. So all may covet the gift of convincing speech in order to touch the unbelieving heart, and the gift of persuasion, to move affections as well as to enlighten the understanding. We may covet knowledge, both of the word and of the works of God, whether of providence or grace. We may desire a measure of that faith, which, on special occasions in which the glory of God or the happiness of men is concerned, goes far beyond the power of natural causes. We may desire an easy flow of speech, a pleasing address surrendered to the will of our Lord, or whatever else would enable us, as we have opportunity, to be useful wherever we are. These gifts we may rightfully desire, but there is still a more desirable, a more excellent way.

That is the way of love. It is loving all men for God's sake. It is a humble, gentle, patient love, which Paul so admirably describes in the following chapter. Without this love, he assures us, all eloquence, knowledge, faith, works, and all sufferings are of no more value in the sight of God than sounding brass or a rumbling cymbal. Without this, they are not of the least benefit toward our eternal salvation. Without this, all we know, all we believe, all we do, all we suffer will profit us nothing in the great day of judgment.

But here, I would take a different view of the text, and point out a more excellent way in another sense. One ancient writer observed there have been from the beginning two kinds of Christians. One lived an innocent life, conforming to the customs and fashions of the world in all things not sinful, doing many good works, abstaining from gross evils, and following the commandments of God. They tried to keep a clear conscience, but did not aim at any particular strictness, being in most things like their neighbors. The other Christians not only kept from all appearance of evil, were diligent in good works of every kind, and kept the commandments of God. They also worked to attain the whole mind that was in Christ, and to be as much like Jesus as possible. In order to do this, they walked in a constant course of universal self-denial, trampling on every pleasure they were not divinely sure was pleasing to God. They took up their cross daily, and tried unceasingly to enter in at the straight gate. They spared no pains to arrive at the summit of Christian holiness, leaving the first principles of the doctrine of Christ to go on to perfection, to know completely the love of God that passes knowledge, and to be filled with all the fullness of God.

From my experience and observation, I am inclined to think that whoever is saved—redeemed by the blood of Jesus—has the choice of walking in the higher or the lower path. I believe the Holy Spirit at that time sets before him the more excellent way and encourages him to walk in it. He inspires all to choose the narrowest path in the narrow way, to aspire to the heights and depths of holiness, and take on the entire image of God. If this offer is not accepted, one imperceptibly declines into the lower order of Christians. In that lower order, one still goes on in what may be called a good way, serving God in a fashion, and finding mercy at the end of life, through the blood of the covenant.

I do not wish to discourage those who serve God in a small way. Simply, I would like for them to keep going. I encourage them to come up higher. Without thundering hell and damnation in their ears, or condemning the path on which they walk—by telling them it is the way that leads to destruction—I will try to point out what is, in every respect, a more excellent way.

Please remember, those who walk on the lower Christian road are not on the road to hell. But this much I know, they will not have so high a place in heaven as they would have had if they had chosen the better path. Will this be a small loss, having fewer stars in the crown of glory? Will it be a little thing to have a lower place in the kingdom of the Father? Certainly there will be no sorrow in heaven. There, all tears will be wiped from our eyes; but if it were possible for grief to enter there, we should grieve at such irreparable loss. Irreparable then, but not now. Now, by the grace of God, we may choose the more excellent way. Let us now compare this with the way in which most Christians walk.

The Typical Versus the More Excellent Way

Start with the beginning of the day. It is the manner of most Christians to rise at eight or nine in the morning, after having lain in bed eight or nine, if not more, hours. I do not say now, as I was very apt to do fifty years ago, that all who indulge themselves in this manner are on the way to hell. But neither can I say they are on the way to heaven, denying themselves and taking up their cross daily.

I am sure there is a more excellent way to promote health, both of body and mind. From an observation of more than sixty years, I have learned that healthy men require an average of six to seven hours of sleep, and healthy women a little more. I know this amount of sleep to be most advantageous to the body as well as the soul. It is preferable to any medicine I have known. It is, therefore, undoubtedly the most excellent way, in defiance of fashion and custom, to take just as much sleep as experience proves our natural requirement. This is indisputably most conducive both to bodily and spiritual health.

Should you refuse to walk in this way simply because it is difficult? With men it is impossible, but all things are possible with God, and by His grace, all things will be possible to you. Just continue constant in prayer, and you will find this not only possible but easy. It is far easier to rise early regularly than to do it only sometimes, but you must begin right. To rise early, you must go to sleep early. Decide, unless something out of the ordinary occurs, to go to bed at a regular hour. The difficulty of it will soon end, but the advantage of it will remain forever.

Most Christians, as soon as they rise, are accustomed to use some kind of prayer, and probably still use the same form they learned when they were very young. Now, I do not condemn those who do this, though many call that mocking God because they have used the same prayer, without variation, for twenty or thirty years. But surely there is a more excellent way of practicing our private devotions.

What if you were to follow this advice? Consider both your outward and inward state, and vary your prayers accordingly. For instance, suppose your outward state is prosperous—you are in good health, ease, and plenty—among kind relations, good neighbors, and agreeable friends, who love you, and you them. Then your outward state manifestly calls for praise and thanksgiving to God. On the other hand, if you are in a state of adversity—in poverty, in want, in outward distress—in imminent danger, in pain and sickness, then you are clearly called to pour out your soul before God in such prayer as is suited to your circumstances. In like manner you may suit your devotions to your inward state, the present state of your mind. Is your soul in heaviness, either from a sense of sin, or through numerous temptations? Then let your prayer consist of such confessions, petitions, and supplications as are suitable to your distressed state of

mind. On the contrary, if your soul is in peace, are you rejoicing in God? When His consolations are small with you,
then say with the psalmist, "Thou art my God, and I will
praise thee: thou art my God, and I will exalt thee" (Ps.
118:28). Also, when you have time, add to your other devotions a little reading and meditation, and perhaps a psalm
of praise, the natural outpouring of a thankful heart. You
must certainly see that this is a more excellent way than the
poor, dry repetitive form.

Most Christians, after using some prayer, usually apply
themselves to business, their secular calling. Everyone who
has any pretense to being a Christian will do this. It is impossible for an idle man to be a good man, since sloth is
inconsistent with religion. But now consider what end you
undertake and follow in your worldly business. Is it to provide things for yourself and your family? It is a good answer,
as far as it goes, but it does not go far enough. Every heathen
goes as far and does his work for the very same reason. A
Christian must go much further. The purpose of all his labor
is to please God, not to do his own will, but the will of Him
who sent us into the world for this very purpose: to do the
will of God on earth as angels do in heaven. He works for
eternity. A true Christian labors not for the goods that perish, that being the smallest motive. He labors for that which
endures to everlasting life. Is this not a more excellent way?

Again, consider the manner in which you transact your
worldly business. With diligence, I trust. Whatever your
hand finds to do, doing it with all your might, in justice,
rendering to all their due, in every circumstance of life, and
in mercy, doing unto everyone what you would have others
do unto you. But a Christian is called to go still further by
adding piety to justice, mixing in prayer, especially prayer
of the heart, with equal labor. Without this, all his diligence
and justice are no different from that of an honest heathen.
There are many who profess Christianity who are no more
than honest heathens.

Yet again, with what spirit do you pursue your business?

Is it in the spirit of the world or in the spirit of Jesus? Thousands of those who are called good Christians do not understand the question. If you act in the spirit of Jesus, you carry your first commitment through all your work, from first to last. You do everything in the spirit of sacrifice, giving up your will to the will of God. You continually aim, not at ease, pleasure, or riches, not at anything this short-enduring world can give, but only at the glory of God. No one can deny this is the most excellent way of pursuing worldly business.

But the bodies we bear require constant repair, or they will sink into the earth from which they were taken even sooner than nature requires. Daily food is necessary to prevent this, to repair the wearing of life. It was common in the heathen world, when they were about to eat or drink, to pour out a little to the honor of their gods, although their gods were but devils. What if, instead of this, every head of a family, before he sat down to eat and drink, either morning, noon or night, were seriously to ask a blessing from God on what he was about to take? And afterward, seriously to offer thanks to the giver of all his blessings? Would this not be a more excellent way than the same hurried and mumbled words so many count as prayer?

As to the quantity of their food, good people usually do not eat to excess, at least not so far as to make themselves sick, or intoxicated with alcohol. If they take only the amount of plain, cheap, wholesome food that best promotes health both of body and mind, there will be no cause for criticism. A king of France, one day, pursuing the chase, outrode all his company, who, after seeking him some time, found him sitting in a cottage eating bread and cheese. Seeing them, he cried out, "Where have I lived all my life? I never before tasted such good food!" "Sire," said one of them, "you never had such good sauce before, for you were never hungry."

It is true, hunger is a good sauce, but there is one still better: thankfulness. Surely thanksgiving makes any food agreeable. Yours should be seasoned with it at every meal.

Consider every morsel as a pledge of life eternal. Your heavenly Father gives you, in your food, not only a reprieve from death, but a promise that in a little time death shall be swallowed up in eternal victory.

The time of taking our food is also a time of conversation. It is natural to refresh our minds while we refresh our bodies. Consider a little, in what manner most Christians usually talk together. What are the ordinary subjects of their conversation? If it is harmless, as one would hope, there is nothing profane, immodest, untrue, or unkind. There is no tale bearing, backbiting, or evil speaking, so they can praise God for His restraining grace. But there is more than this implied in "ordering our conversation aright."

In order for it to be proper, it is necessary that it is materially good, set on good subjects and not fluttering about everything that occurs. Worldly things are not your business, except when some remarkable event calls for the acknowledgment of the justice or mercy of God. You must, indeed, sometimes talk of worldly things (otherwise we may as well leave the world), but that should be done only so far as is necessary. Then we should return to a better subject. Second, let your conversation be edifying, calculated to edify either the speaker or the hearers or both. It should build them up, as each has particular need, either in faith, or love, or holiness. Third, see that it not only entertains, but in one way or another ministers grace to the hearers. This is a more excellent way of conversing for the glory of the gospel.

We have discussed the more excellent way of directing conversation and business, but we cannot always be intent upon business. Both our bodies and our minds require some relaxation. We need intervals of diversion from business. It is necessary to be very explicit on this, as this point has been greatly misunderstood.

There are various kinds of diversions. Some are almost peculiar to men, such as the sports of the field: hunting, shooting, and fishing, in which not many women are concerned. Others are of a more public nature, used by both sexes, such as races, masquerades, plays, assemblies, balls. Still others are more often found in private houses, such as games, dancing, and music, as well as the reading of plays, novels, romances, newspapers, and poetry. Let those who have nothing better to do keep running the breath out of foxes and hares. Nothing much needs to be said about horse races, since no man of sense will attempt to defend them. It seems a great deal more may be said in defense of seeing a serious tragedy.

I could not, with a clear conscience, defend theater, the epitome of all profaneness and debauchery. Possibly others can. I cannot say much for balls or assemblies, which, though more reputable than masquerades, yet must be conceded to have exactly the same tendency as all public dances. They must have the same tendency unless the same care is taken among modern Christians as was observed among the ancient heathens. In those times, men and women never danced together, but always in separate rooms. This rule was always observed in ancient Greece, and for several ages in Rome, where a woman dancing in company with men would have at once been called a prostitute. Of playing games, I say the same as of seeing plays. I could not do it with a clear conscience. But I am not obliged to pass sentence on those who are of another mind. I leave them to their own Master. Before Him, let them stand or fall.

Suppose all these, as well as the reading of plays, novels, newspapers, and the like, are quite innocent diversions. Are there not more excellent ways of relaxation for those who love or fear God? Men of fortune may divert themselves by cultivating and improving their lands, by planting their grounds, by laying out, continuing, and perfecting their gardens and orchards. At other times they may visit and converse with the most serious and sensible of their neighbors, or they may visit the sick, the poor, the widows and the fatherless in their affliction. They desire to divert themselves indoors. There they may read useful history, pious and elegant poetry, theology or natural philosophy. If there is time, you may divert yourself by music, and perhaps by philosophical experiments. But above all, when you have once learned the use of prayer, you will find that it will fill your heart and mind until in every area of life it will spread through all your work, and wherever you are, whatever you do, it will embrace you on every side. Then you will be able to say boldly, "My boredom is gone. I live only to serve my God, and know only Jesus."

One last point to be considered is the use of money. How do most Christians use this? There is a more excellent way. Most Christians usually set apart something yearly, perhaps a tenth or even an eighth of their income, from whatever source, for charitable uses. I have known a few who said, like Zaccheus, "Lord, the half of my goods I give to the poor." I wish God would multiply those friends of mankind, those general benefactors.

But, besides those who have a stated rule, there are many who give large sums to the poor, especially when they hear a striking tale of distress told to them in dramatic terms.

I praise God for all of you who act in this manner. May you never be weary of well-doing. May God restore sevenfold to you what you give. But there is still a more excellent way.

You may consider yourself one in whose hands God has placed a large part of His goods to be disposed of according to His direction. And His direction is that you should look upon yourself as one of a certain number of indigent persons who are to be provided for out of that portion of His goods with which you are entrusted. You have two advantages over the rest. One, it is more blessed to give than to receive; and the other, that you are to serve yourself first, and the others afterward. This is the light in which you are to see yourself and them. But to be more particular, if you have no family, after you have provided for yourself, give away all that remains. This was the practice of all the young men at Oxford who were called Methodists. For example, one of them had thirty dollars. He lived on twenty-eight, and gave away two. The next year he had sixty dollars, and still lived on twenty-eight, and gave away thirty-two. The third year he received ninety dollars and gave away sixty-two. The fourth year he received a hundred and twenty. Still he lived as before, on twenty-eight, so he gave ninety-two to the poor. This was a more excellent way.

If you have a family, seriously consider before God how much each member of it needs in order to have what is necessary for life and godliness. In general, do not allow them less, nor much more, than you allow yourself. This being done, fix your purpose to gain no more. I charge you in the name of God, do not increase your substance. As it comes daily or yearly, so let it go, otherwise you lay up treasures upon earth. This our Lord as flatly forbids as murder or adultery. By doing it, therefore, you would store up for yourself wrath against the day of wrath, and revelation of the righteous judgment of God. Even if you were not forbidden, how could anyone, on principles of reason, spend money in a way that God may possibly forgive, instead of spending it in a way that He will certainly reward?

There is no reward in heaven for what you stored. There is a reward for what is given out. Every dollar put into the earthly bank is sunk because it earns no interest in heaven. But every dollar you give to the needy is put into the bank of heaven. It will bring glorious interest, which accumulates through eternity. Who among you is wise and endued with knowledge? Resolve this day, this hour, this moment, the Lord assisting, to choose "the more excellent way" in all things. Keep to it steadily, in regard to sleep, prayer, work, food, conversation, diversions, and particularly to the employment of that important talent, money. Let your heart answer to the call of God: "From this moment, God being my helper, I will store up no more treasure upon the earth. One thing I will do is to lay up treasure in heaven. I will render unto God the things that are God's. I will give Him all my goods, and all my heart."